# Rebound Forward:
## Second Edition

## Randy Brown

© Randy Brown, Author ~ "Rebound Forward"
Second Edition

ISBN-13: 978-1-944662-24-0

May 2018

Published by Open eye Press

Winning Proof: Michelle Hill, Collaborator

Cover Design: Amy Lambert, @eighmmie

During 2016 the author sited Dictionary.com

Printed in the United States of America

# Dedication

This book is dedicated to our two girls, Meredith and Natalie. They left us much too early but enriched our lives each day they were with us.

We rejoice in knowing we will see them soon.

Meredith, November 28, 1988-November 29, 1992
Natalie, April 8, 1994-February 2, 1998

# Table of Contents

# Acknowledgments

This book started innocently enough as a journal to help pass the time for two years at Butner Federal Prison, North Carolina. The handwritten version of "Rebound Forward" became typewritten thanks to a 1980s version of the Smith-Corona typewriter. I used my Federal ID to borrow the type-writer and while writing, bought quite a number of black cartridges through the commisary. I hate to think of the bill I rang up purchasing cartridges and stamps as I banged out these pages daily. The looks I got from my compadres were priceless.

———

My mom, Nan, did wonders raising four kids and she remains my rock today. My brothers Roger and Rick, along with my sister Renee, have always been there for me and my family. We've endured a lot together and know there will be more, but we'll do whatever it is together. Daughters Claire and Jane are bright lights in my life and their humor, inspiration, support and love is precious. They are gifts from God and the center of my life. Natalie and Meredith are so proud of them.

My dad, Bob, passed away in 2012 and was an award-winning sports writer for the Fort Dodge Messenger. His influence runs through every page of this book. During my formative years, I thanked him for driving past Ames on so many football Saturdays to experience the magic of Kinnick Stadium and Iowa City. If you're a Brown, you're a Hawk for life. He and my brother Rick have won countless awards for superior journalism and both are members of the Media Hall of Fame in the University of Iowa's Kinnick Stadium press box in Iowa City. I guess I got their crumbs.

So many close friends have made up the supportive writing team I've leaned on for the past several years. Leading the charge is David Staff, senior pastor of Christ Community Church in Ames. David wrote me a letter every day I was away at Butner. "Every day!" Whether on the phone, in person, in the mail or just in their thoughts, this list contains the names of people who have been instrumental to me in this project; Kirk Ferentz, Tim Floyd, Orv Salmon, Bob Sundvold, Gary Garner, Lute Olson, Steve Burgason, Bob Ostrich, John Engelman, Cedric Barnes, Howie Gauthier, Tom Crean, Tom Billeter, Jeff Rutter, Ben Jacobson, Rus Bradburd, Hans Halbur, Nick Johnson, Tom Pipines, Carey Burkett, Todd Sexe, Mark Behrens, Bart Warren, Tom Anderson, Jay Christensen, Dan O'Brion, Herman Richter, Jessica Hoy, Paul Shirley, Casey McClain, Rich Glas, Greg McDermott, Dan Hipsher, Rick Neilsen, Scott Howard, Greg Lansing, Denny Kuiper, Scott Nelson, Dave Schlabaugh, Don Showalter, Lon Kruger, John Barbier, Rod Bodholdt, Jeff Grummer, Jack Burns, Matt Youngs, Mike Green, Dan McCarney—all coaching members of my Elite Mentoring Program, and the Huseman family.

Dutch Huseman, a legendary Iowa high school basketball coach in Fort Dodge, was my coaching idol from the time I could pull a ball from the rack. I watched his practices as a youngster with amazement and thought maybe I could do that when I grew up. He represented everything good about the game; perspective, respect, competition, toughness, and sportsmanship. Dutch passed away in 2016 at the age of 93. I miss our hoop talks.

Finally, I want to share a relational rarity. Bart Warren, a.k.a. Hone, and I have been best friends since forever. His mom, Becky, was a rabid Hawkeye fan, held a special place in my heart, and was best friends with my mom, Nan. Becky left us on August 20th, 2017, but her love remains to the end. How often do you hear of sons and moms being best friends? Beck, you helped me through every loss as if I was your own. I love you, miss you, and thank you for your spirit every day.

My book support staff includes Michelle Hill (owner of Winning Proof), Drew Becker(publisher, Open eye Press),

Amy Lambert (cover designer), and countless reviewers.

Michelle is the actual hero who helped make this book a reality. One day on LinkedIn, I noticed her name and title. She was listed as a ghostwriter and book collaborator in the sports book industry. I reached out to learn more and a conversation soon began. The result was an explosion of commitment and accountability that helped me pick up those 305 pages I had etched out while at Butner. After collaborating with Michelle, I began assembling a new puzzle. Without this encounter, I doubt any progress could have been made. Ever since, she has been an excellent supporter and professional.

Drew Becker worked with me to get the manuscript ready for print and also helped me through the publishing experience. As with all books, there were unseen challenges, as in life, and he helped navigate through those enabling the book to be published in this second edition the way I wanted it to be presented.

Amy Lambert is one of the most special people I've ever met. She entered my life at a fragile time when I needed her gentle spirit the most. Amy is amazingly talented as witnessed by her work on the cover and the graphics my books contains. She was my sounding board throughout the process and continues to be. Amy reminds me often to be good to myself and stand tall. Thanks.

I'm very blessed to have met all three ladies and they are as much a part of this project as I am. If meeting supportive, caring, and non-judgmental people are part of the book writing process, I think I've got a dozen more projects in mind.

*Thanks to all,*
*Randy*

# Introduction

One of the real pleasures of coaching in the upper echelons of college basketball is found in the final minutes of the game. Hours of preparation, practice, tape sessions, travel, stress, and loss of sleep all go into each game. The bigger the game, the more exaggerated the preparation. The bigger the game, the more agonizing the last ticks of the clock.

A close, intense game that dips below one minute is what competition is all about – all previous decisions, turnovers and bad calls are forgotten. The final moments are magnified and mean the world, or so it seems. A timeout offers the opportunity to settle your troops and lay out the plan for winning, and as the players step away from the huddle, only thoughts of positive results are allowed.

In a tied situation, my preference is to defend our goal. Laser-focused on the rim first, ball second, and players third, we operate from a position of strength. If the opponent is strategizing for the last shot, in a flash of movement, a dozen things can go wrong and my stomach turns summersaults. We build our program's success on defense. Therefore, we are confident. Coaches and players scream, "One stop; all we need is one stop."

I recall many such situations – they all play in slow motion. I've reviewed them hundreds of times. The home crowd rises to its feet and fills every square inch of air with deafening volume; the beauty of the moment is when the volume turns to a deathly silence.

The opponent designs a play and puts it in motion.

There is a winning look in each defender's eyes. Knowing grins and clenched fists say it all. It's a look of confidence and conviction.

Each player spreads his feet wider than usual and slaps the floor to demonstrate unity and determination, then effortlessly, as the action begins, they shuffle their feet and communicate with ease. It's the perfect defensive effort unfolding in front of me. I realize there is nothing I can do to affect the outcome. I helplessly watch from the sidelines - I know my work is now done. The players must execute. Each player's mind reviews the difficulty of fall conditioning, the near misses, and the pain of past defeat. Everything within their power will be executed to avoid that helpless, draining feeling of a game lost.

Our defenders work as a unit, a dominant collection of wills and desires. Once the shot is taken – with only a few ticks left on the clock – the world seems to stop. Stop cold! In the field of college basketball, the outcome of the shot can label you a winner or a loser. Whether or not the ball fits into the fixed orange cylinder dictates our mere humanness – at least for that moment – it becomes a permanent stamp that signifies the victory in papers across the country. An unexplainable feeling rushes through my body as the ball inches toward its destination. The thump of my heart pounds, the same beats shared by the coaches sitting on both sides of me.

The feeling of a dagger piercing my heart is immediate if the opponent prevails. It can happen despite all good intentions, effort, and hope. As deflating as that feeling is, the opposite is much greater. As the ball bounces off the rim and into the waiting hands of one of our players, my body erupts sensations known only to those who have labored on the sidelines. I'm most certain that there's no feeling quite like the euphoria of winning a key basketball game.

The usual raucous Hilton Coliseum crowd was silent on this late January Big 12 tilt in 2002. History was imminent as Iowa State's Tyray Pearson stepped to the line to shoot a one-and-one with 00:59 remaining and a one-point lead. It was the usual ultra-competitive game between Kansas and Iowa State. Kansas was in the unfamiliar position of being behind late in the game. It would take a missed one-and-one by Pearson and a heroic three-pointer bomb by Jeff Boschee to steal the Jayhawk win.

The post-game handshakes were routine although my handshake with Roy Williams had a different feel to it. It was the first time in six games that his team managed to beat our relentless, tough band of defenders. I'll always cherish those five grips in victory with the future Hall of Fame coach. I know Roy to be a good guy, an excellent basketball coach and someone who would become a future neighbor. Who would have thought? Fast forward to April 2005. Combing through a pile of recent papers, I found an article on Roy Williams and his National Championship North Carolina Tar Heels. They had just captured the 2005 crown with a 75-70 win over Illinois in St. Louis.

———

A long pause, then a steady gaze at nothing. I imagined a celebration but had no reason for joy. It wasn't handshaking time anymore; this was prison time. That afternoon as I walked the one-third mile rough gravel track at Butner Federal Prison, I gazed to the southwest. With the University of North Carolina in Chapel Hill just 22 miles away I could almost hear the victory parade ensue.

Adversity is inevitable and can be a vicious animal. In one fleeting second, it can level a person. The pain that accompanies suffering is blinding – physically, mentally, and emotionally draining. In an instant, all joy is sucked out of life. It changes you, the world and everything around it. The past pushes you to create a new present, sometimes wanted and other times not, it's simply a reality of our time on earth.

My 59-year journey has encompassed numerous highs and lows. I'm not talking about losing basketball games, because I've lost my share. Hitting bottom and facing my own mortality define my lows. Some I caused through selfishness and poor decision-making and other situations just happened.

Through these pages you will read about my struggles with addiction, depression, stress, losing jobs, divorce, and prison. Add to that the deaths of our two beautiful girls, ages three and a half and four. Facing the harsh reality of these life-defining experiences changed me forever. I found myself wallowing in a seemingly hopeless abyss. Could I have avoided some of these life events? Surely. Did I? No. Why? You'll find out the consequences of my behaviors and the changes I would have made. I will advise you not to make the same poor choices I did.

Proper responses and resulting decisions can strengthen you like nothing else. Forgiveness, second chances, acceptance, gratitude, faith, sense of humor, perspective, humility, and selflessness will all result from making good choices in the wake of devastation. Isn't it worth it? I can answer that for you with a resounding, "YES!"

There are positive results that stem from adversity and I will share those with you, too. I'll illustrate how adversity can be defeated with a strong presence of friends, family, and faith. When you learn how to respond to adversity the right way – you gain strength that helps you when the next circumstance hits. That strength then becomes like layers of armor you add to your body, mind, emotions, and spirit. But there is a warning I must offer. Dealing with difficult situations does not always yield a positive outcome. This is not a Pollyannaish attempt to minimize the serious nature of tragedy. It would be a beautiful world if everything averse turned out rosy. The world has other plans. The result may be positive and add to your resilience or it may grind you down to a pulp. Be warned that poor choices can destroy you. Anything is possible when the tornados of life strike. This is not an attempt at shared pity or a release from responsibility. Any hint at feeling sorry for me and my path in life is futile.

Rebounding is not for the weak. It is physical, demanding, and relentless. Great rebounders seek the ball at all costs. My strength and hope come from being transparent and sharing my journey. The more I share, the stronger I get, and the more rebounds I gain. The more balls I snatch off the rim, the more I can share with others. I know there are so many people out there who have heartache and pain that is imprisoned inside of them. My hope is that sharing my message will open them to the possibilities of freedom and optimism. Even after 600 games, I will continue to seek the next rebound. I now realize I have enough and I can freely give to those in need, even if it's just one person. With that nudge, I'm confident you will rebound forward!

*Rebound Forward* will challenge your thinking on adversity. You will learn how your choices can become the world's greatest learning tool to launch you forward in life. In reading my story, my hope is that you will gain insight into a life that has been touched by adversity more than most. Ultimately, my goal is for you to identify the choices and skills you can take as you face future difficulties. You will find yourself reflecting on your past, most likely identifying times when you, too, fell short. You can decide if facing reality or running is your preferred response. If this book allows you to make one good decision in adversity, then my venture has been a worthy one.

I know one thing for sure. When the going gets tough, don't run! A strong man must stand resolved in the face of strong winds and turn a bad *anything* into a good *something*. I'm here to tell you that it CAN be done, and I hope my life's whirlwinds encourage you in the midst of the adversities that will surely arise during your journey on earth.

*Life is adversity.*
*Adversity is life.*
*You have a choice.*
*Rebound Forward.*
*This is my story.*

∞

# Chapter One
# Lean on Me

*"Circumstances break men's bones; it has never been shown that they break men's optimism."*

### ~ G. K. Chesterton

"You take it out," I said, as Bart Warren grabbed the ball out of the net after yet another field goal by Marshalltown High School's Craig DeVolder. "Play some D, Knut," Bart barked, as he carefully stepped out of bounds. He slapped the ball hard, venting his frustrations on our team's defense in this tight game. As his starting teammate in the Fort Dodge High School Dodger backcourt during the 1975—1976 season, I alone recognized the opportunity Bart created by taking the ball out of bounds. We secretly played a game within the game about who would take it out. Many times the ball swished through the net and bounced helplessly on the hardwood, the two of us equidistant from it, each pretending the other was closer.

Head Coach Jim Friest's offense dictated that the two guards were responsible for getting the ball inbounds and up the floor. Both of us wanted that job of advancing the ball up the floor, as we directed the team from the point guard position. There is something special about being the quarterback, the pitcher, and the point guard. All eyes are on you, and your team's success can usually be tied directly to your productivity, leadership, and decision-making.

Bart, an all-state pitcher, and future college pitcher was also the Dodger quarterback for two years. Clad in tight football pants, free of hip pads, he led the gridiron hopes efficiently down every opponent's field in the Big 8 Conference. A born leader and take-charge guy, Bart won the 1976 Schultz Award, citing the most exceptional male athlete at Fort Dodge High School.

So, as we continued to battle the Marshalltown High Bobcats on the court, it was to my surprise that Bart took the ball out of bounds on this occasion. After cutting to shake the Bobcat defender, I caught the ball and faced the entire court without using my dribble. All I knew is that as the game progressed, each possession grew in importance. Frozen in time, I thought, "How many times did I dream of the chance to help the Dodgers win a game?" Being guarded aggressively by Doug Ray, I began to advance the ball up the floor, making a move to the middle of the floor near my defender.

Suddenly I noticed Bart's defender sprinting at me for a run-and-jump double team. In an instant, instead of hitting Bart, who was flanked 15 feet to my right, I decided to change my dribble with a right-to-left crossover, veering to the left sideline. Open for a moment, I flew by the Marshalltown bench with Ray in hot pursuit over my right shoulder. Eyeing Dan Siekmann in his position on the left wing, I prepared to deliver a pass to him down the left sideline. BOOM! My left foot mysteriously slipped, as if I had been on a newly waxed wooden floor in some historic art museum. My body flew airborne, the ball helplessly slipping out of my hands. As gravity pulled me downward, the ball was within reach.

It seemed that I could virtually see every dimple on that Wilson Jet basketball. Now directly in front of our bench, my only hope was to bat it forward to Siekmann who waited for my pass. Just before hitting the floor, I tapped it with all the leverage and strength I had left. As if in a slow-moving dream, I saw the ball deflect off my right index finger out of bounds. Hitting the floor hard, my two protruding pelvis bones took the brunt of the crash, immediately stinging. I lay there motionless for an instant, flooded by knowledge of what a turnover could mean to the outcome of this vital game.

Before getting up, from less than five feet away, I heard the angry voice of Coach Friest, screaming, "Get up! Get off that floor!" I raised my head to do just that when a hand extended to help me up. "Keep your head up, Brownie," offered Bart, who arrived quickly to the scene of the accident.

The tension-filled game, interrupted by a strange free-throw rule interpretation favoring the opponent, caused our visitors, the Bobcats, to ultimately win the game. Crushed over the importance of that game and the recognition of my costly turnover, I sat forever in the locker room after all my teammates had left. My dad, having concluded his post-game interviews and duties, patted me on the head and offered encouragement. I s-l-o-w-l-y put on my clothes, laced up my shoes and walked out. Together, the sportswriter and I, his son, exited the empty gym together, as we had been doing for years.

Being offered a hand to get up off the floor that night, how could I have imagined the power of the one there to assist me? I had known Bart Warren since grade school. We played sports together and had become friends through those developmental years, continuing our friendship into junior high and high school. From Bart and his parents, Jim and Becky, there was always a sense of sincerity, comfort, and unconditional acceptance. I can hear Bart saying to me, "Hey, listen pal, I'll always be there for you, okay? Don't worry about anything – I mean it. All you have to do is call, no matter what time, and I'll be there. Always!"

------

*"A true friend never gets in your way unless you are going down."*

**~ Arnold H. Glasow**

The distorted loudspeaker boomed, "Randall Brown, Maryland Unit, report to the visiting room." As I popped up out of my top bunk to my feet and checked for my BOP Identification card, I reflected on a powerful thought: *Bart is here to visit me.* I wondered how many times he has been there to support me. Twenty-nine years separated us from that painful Marshalltown game. On this day though, the same two guys came together in a place far from Dodger Fieldhouse.

*Rebound Forward*

The same hand that pulled me off the sweaty floor nearly three decades ago extended to me once again, this time as we emotionally embraced in the visitation room of North Carolina's Butner Federal Correctional Institution. This embrace felt even better than the last. The grip was the same, only the venue had changed. The strength in his hug said, "Hey pal, I'm here for you and I'll always be here for you." In that moment, we could just as well have been putting for birdies on a well-manicured green as hanging out in a prison visitation room. All that mattered was that he was there to pick me up again.

————

A recent conversation with my mom brought up a jewel of her guidance as a supportive and loving mother. She asked, "What's the best advice I ever gave you?"

When I was 12 years old, she talked with me about my friends and how important they were. I agreed that I had friends, some from school, church, outdoor activities, and sports. She wanted to know who my best friends were, and I spouted off two or three. She continued to dig, asking, "Do any of your friends do things you know are wrong, yet you still hang out with them?"

"Yes, I guess," I responded. My mother explained that we all make mistakes, but she expressed that when I choose to hang out with a group of boys who are getting into trouble, then she gets concerned – and I should too. That stuck with me for a while, until our follow-up talk.

"Remember when we talked about your friends the other day?" she asked. I nodded. Then she shared with me that at 11:30 p.m. the previous night a friend who had just lost her husband called in tears. She was reaching out to a few of her closest friends because she was so sad and angry at God. "I was so glad I talked to her," my mom explained, "because she desperately needed to share her grief." 24/7 ?

————

*"I'll lean on you and you lean on me and we'll be okay."*

**~ Dave Matthews**

Her wise words continued. "If you have good friends and keep those friends as you grow up, they will always be there for you when tragic things happen in your life. So, choose your friends wisely. My older brother, Rick, had a group of friends who were the kind I looked up to. I wanted a group just like he did. "You just never know, some of them may be friends forever," my mom said. Boy was she right. To this day, her advice is the best I've ever been given!

Friends are formed in pockets based on age and environment. Elementary friends seem like they'll be there forever, but they usually fade out by middle school. Other kids seem to have something that makes the friendship just click. These are the ones who you gather with initially and sometimes endure for the long haul.

Many times, in conversation, I've referenced my friends and their value in my life. It leads to a curious look and a question about where my friends are from. Most people guess they are from work, church, or that they're neighbors. I proudly state, "No, these are my high school buddies, we've been tight forever." Most people say they've lost touch with their high school friends years ago. I also make a point to share another key aspect of friendship: Facing adversity as life moves on will bring out your Band of Brothers like none else.

Seventh grade basketball was a dream-like experience, as were the next two seasons. Coaching can impact young people like no other and I was no exception. Ken Sawyer was a no-nonsense coach with a bark that could frighten any 13-year-old. Driven by fundamentals, he possessed a gentler side and carried a great, dry humor. A true educator, as a social studies teacher and coach in every sport the administration could plug him into, Coach Sawyer had my full admiration.

The beginning of friendships began in earnest during that season, marked by its memorable 6:00 a.m. practices in the frigid cold. By the time we were thawed out, a quick, hard practice was over, and we headed to homeroom. I never quite fathomed just how fast those practices went by.

Ken remained a friend throughout my career and was thrilled I decided to become a coach. We need more Ken Sawyers in education. Men like Ken, who passed in 2016, can have a profound impact on young, impressionable young men like me.

Kraig Knutson and Dan Siekmann, our center and forward respectively, and I, would play together through our high school careers, and Knutson would join me at Iowa Central Community College in Fort Dodge for two years after we graduated. Kraig and I became an extension of each other due to countless hours on cement surfaces, 12 months a year. He is responsible for my hearing loss at an early age due to his massively powerful Marantz amp and four Bose 901 speakers. Music, hoops, and friendship. You can't beat it!

A company of buddies was beginning to form. Missing from our 7th hoop team was talented Bart Warren, who chose wrestling for a winter. He joined us on the 8th grade team and the unit of Warren, Brown, Siekmann and Knutson would play every game together for the next five years.

———

*"Do not judge me by my successes. Judge me by how many times I fell down and got back up again."*

**~ Nelson Mandela**

Dazed, I sat in the east bleachers of Iowa State University's Hilton Coliseum in December of 1997. Unemployed and 40, I spaced out and stared at the game in front of me. Dave Wilson, a fellow Fort Dodger, and one year my junior sat down next to me. We sat and talked as the Cyclones were doing battle against the legendary Pete Carill's Princeton Tigers.

As usual, the unique pass, space, and back-cut Princeton offense added years to Cyclone coach Tim Floyd's life. A defensive genius, Floyd would battle for 40 minutes to win the gut-wrenching game. After a flurry of excitement on the floor, I asked Dave, "How many of your buddies went to school here when you were at ISU?" He mentioned a few names, but most had fallen away through the years. He then asked about my friends when I went to Iowa.

"Well, there were a few," I told him. "Hone, Eliot, Krata, Keek, Bog, Torf, Beej, J-Bomb, Doc, Rog, Stump, Cakes, Tundro, Siek, Harry, Richie, Jimmy K, Heimy, Willie, Coley, and..." The list had 20 names by the time I finished. It could have included Bear, Stretch, and Burk due to their frequent presence in Iowa City. Roger, my brother, and two years younger, played golf at Iowa and was my apartment roommate. The rest of the group didn't play sports but did a lot of running; from bar to bar that is. As you can tell by this list, having a nickname in Fort Dodge, Iowa is just part of being from Dodge. Other than a nail biter won by Coach Tim Floyd's Cyclones that's all I remember about that night.

On my two-hour drive from Ames back to Cedar Falls, I thought about that group in school together at the University of Iowa. I realized that we had always hung out in packs. Like a secret society of brothers, we had stayed intact through the days of youth and then into our 20s. But it hadn't stopped there.

I pulled my unstable 1985 Toyota Camry onto a favorite gravel farm road and spent a long time staring up at the stars, comfortably perched on my back trunk. Midlife has a way of making you look back at things you didn't think you had time to revisit in your 30's. I pondered the years full of ups and downs, moving from city to city, pursuing a dream in the midst of loss, yet always keeping tabs on my guys.

They seem to call or write at just the perfect time. They appear without asking for their presence. Whether checking in or comforting you at a critical time, the right friends are a gift.

Speaking in front of an audience, large or small, is a challenge. Fortunately, over the years as a coach I've spoken hundreds of times. It's not being in front of a crowd that creates apprehension; many times, it's the subject matter. When I decided to turn my mess into a message in 2006, I had to accept the fact that the subject matter would be tricky based on the audience. When speaking to a college class, a church men's group, or a small transparent gathering, I knew I would be putting a piece of myself and my experiences on the table.

Such was the case when I was asked to speak to a men's group at a church in Des Moines a few years back. As I surveyed the group of 60 men I realized they were like any other group I had spoken to. In most of the settings I speak in, the audience can be described as quiet and curious. As I began telling my story to this particular men's group, I begin to talk about relationships and how they can make all the difference in times of need. My eyes glanced right to left and I saw someone who caused me to pause. I stopped. I took a deep breath, followed by emotions that only special memories can invoke. "Hi, Larry," I offered. "Hey, guys, I need to take a detour for a second."

"My friend Larry Burkett is here and I'd be remiss if I didn't mention his son, Carey." Tearing up now, I said, "Larry, your son has meant the world to me. He is the most compasssionate, understanding friend anyone could ever dream of having. In my darkest times, he has been there for me. As I look at you I see him and his smile, and his arms offering a giant hug of love and comfort. There is nothing in the world I would give in exchange for his friendship. I just wanted to tell you that." Larry and I shared a tear in the midst of 60 men. We greeted each other after my talk and his bear hug nearly broke me in two. Tears flowed again as I thanked him and his wife, Barb, for raising such an awesome friend.

Get close to people who will be there for you – and you for them. Then, now, and forever. Friends for life.

# Chapter Two
## Door to Door

*"The same wind blows on us all; the winds of disaster, opportunity and change. Therefore, it is not the blowing of the wind, but the setting of the sails that will determine our direction in life."*

**~ Jim Rohn**

At the intersection of two less traveled roads sat a senior man. His head was bowed toward the ground and he was in deep thought. Or maybe he was sleeping. I walked up to the man and greeted him. The old fellow offered me a bright smile followed by a gentle hug.

"What brings you out today?" I asked, sensing he was in need of companionship and had a story to share. We sat on a nearby bench as he took off his hat and set it down with care. From inside his tattered coat he pulled out a dirty, well-used notebook and trusty pencil and began to tell me about his childhood. As an eight-year-old, he went door to door selling chickens, eggs, and vegetables. Often his grandmother would join him and on the way, they talked. The topic was different each time, but he listened as if his life hung on every word. One rainy, gray day they headed out on their route. At one house, he heard a woman moaning and crying painfully, the kind of sobbing you can't ignore. Later he asked Granny about the woman and the reason for her sadness. She paused before answering, knowing that the answer would be a pivotal truth in his life.

She said, "God doesn't discriminate when it comes to handing out pain. Throughout our lives, events can bring joy and sorrow. No person is exempt from adversity, that's just a part of life. Son, you can knock on every door in every town for the rest of your life and ask if adversity has touched their lives.

I think you know the answer, but if you are still curious, try it out sometime."

Even after so many years, the determined man was still curious about life and its difficulties. He was intrigued by the fact some people seemed to have it made while others were constantly down on their luck. Now he was on his last fact-finding adventure as his doctor had said his days were numbered. He set himself on finding the truth: Does adversity touch everyone?

He knew the types of misfortune life offers, but he was curious about the reaction or response to difficult times.

"The first home that I visited during this final adventure had their share of suffering for sure. The blank-faced man who opened the door described an automobile accident three years prior, which took his wife. He had become a recluse and didn't venture much outside his home after her death. Once full of life, his days were packed with gardening, bike riding, playing bridge, and fishing. Now he was only a shell of a man."

"Next was a cancer story that brought me to tears," the old man continued, his head bowed down as he sighed and looked toward the ground. "Their child had been sick since birth and lived to the age of almost three before she succumbed to the dreaded disease." He walked away from the home studying the cracks in the cement as he wept and shook his head.

The man trudged on and discovered a tragic story of gambling. Following layoffs at work, the husband lost his job of 37 years at the local foundry. Devastated, he began gambling, carefully at first, not enough to be noticed. Losing escalated the activity until his losses were hundreds a day or more. He entered treatment but returned to the casino. This cycle continued three times until he became bedridden and passed at the age of 86.

In the far reaches of a cul-de-sac, an eight-year-old boy with a bright-eyed face opened the door. Being the only one home at the time, he reluctantly spoke with the old man. The man, expecting a clean, fresh slate from the boy who opened the door, was knocked back when he heard of the loss of the boy's grandmother one-week prior. The boy was still a bit shaken by it all, making the situation uncomfortable. The child hesitated, then continued with a story of another boy from his Sunday school who had been killed while riding his bike the previous summer. Heartbroken, the senior man thanked the boy and slowly walked the uneven sidewalk to the street. "I should have skipped that house," he muttered.

A beautiful, well-manicured home loomed large as he rang the doorbell. Could this be the family that had escaped the life curse of hardship? Maybe he had solved the puzzle on the first day of his task.

A man in a wheelchair opened the door and barked orders to leave the property immediately. His wife apologized for her husband, explaining that he hadn't been the same after learning of a rare muscle defect that deemed him wheelchair bound.

One after another, after another, the man repeated the pattern. He ended his first day exhausted but still hoping to find the perfect family the next day.

A week passed; then a month. Stamina was an issue for the old guy, but he labored like a champion, committed to his research. Fall turned to winter, and that slowed his pace substantially. He spent hours combing through books and journals reading up on the cause and reaction to the bad things that occur in life. Not even in the vast library he frequented that winter did he find what he was looking for.

*"Before my father was killed, my life was impenetrable. Bad things happened to other people. I thought I was immune from anything like that."*

**~ Steve Kerr, Head Coach,
Golden State Warriors**

Spring brought hope and a sense of newness. He was upbeat as he started where he had left off. Again, the results were the same. A few months later after exhaustive work, he threw in the towel. Though his research did not cover every front door in the world, he knew from his experience that no one is free from adversity. Freedom came over him as he realized we are all part of a global fraternity. Staring up into the clouds he clearly said, "The same wind blows on us all!" Knowing that we are all subject to a measure of adversity and hardship, it leaves each of us with a choice to make when it hits us.

The old-timer kept immaculate notes concerning the devastating result of tough times. It became apparent that people make their decisions based on a variety of reasons. People are different, and each of us has a history that guides our future choices.

As he packed up his tattered notebook for the last time, he whispered, "Be kind to everyone, because everyone is fighting some sort of battle." ☺ —

# Chapter Three
# "Scarred but Smarter"
(title of song by Kevn Kinney)

*"Failure is either a great educator or a*
*magnificent train wreck!"*

**~ Unknown**

Three children sit closely as they play with dozens of toys. They play, exchange toys, and appear happy. Chaos arises as a toy, one of 37, becomes the target of two eager kids. The tug-of-war ensues, and the winner clutches the prize. The defeated party screams, "That's not fair, he took my truck."

What is fair? Does it exist? If it does, where did it come from and is it a birthright? Is every person immediately given a certificate at birth that states, "Life is fair and life is also unfair, you decide?" Of course not. It begs the question, "If there is no such thing as fair then is unfair fictitious too?" As life has its way with us, no matter what happens, it is neither. Things happen in life. Get used to it. Leaning on the security of unfair gives us an out and a quick escape from acceptance.

Life throws punches of death, sickness, job loss, divorce, and tsunamis at us. We shouldn't be surprised in the least when these things happen. Events might make us sad but why fight something that is going to happen anyway? It may appear in a different package each time but it's always around the corner. As singer/songwriter Kevn Kinney sings, "Nobody said it would be fair, they warned you before you went out there." Maybe this perspective will help you prepare for a life with adversity.

*"Fair is a place where they judge pigs."*

**~ Unknown**

Fair- doesn't exist

Scott Peck, in his landmark book "The Road Less Traveled," hits the target on the reality of this thing called life: *"Most do not fully see this truth that life is difficult. Instead, they moan incessantly, noisily, or subtly, about the enormity of their problems, their burdens, and their difficulties as if life were generally easy, as if life should be easy."*

Adversity is a catch-all phrase that connotes a condition marked by misfortune, hardship, calamity, fate, or distress. It is an unfortunate event or circumstance. Adversity stings initially. It causes that shock and awe sensation. Because it is "not supposed to happen to us." We are knocked back a step or two until we get a chance to pause, reflect and decide how to move forward. Adversity, pain, disappointment, tragedy, and inconceivable events are lifelong companions. Get used to it because they are not going away. You can moan and complain about them, but when you get up the next day, they'll still be there. Life is a birthmark you despise; it was there when you were born and will be a constant in your life until your expiration date.

Adversity comes in all shapes and sizes, and it has many names: hardship, difficulty, obstacle, setback, crisis, failure, or suffering. Regardless of what you call it, it is adversity all the same. In fact, adversity plays no favorites and may strike with an equal vengeance upon your business, your marriage, your health, your family, or any other corner of life. Deal with it!

After the dust settles on tragic news, we all have a choice for our *response* to it. Notice I use the descriptor *respond*, not *react*. A reaction is an instant reaction we form based on instinct and a fight or flight dynamic. Reaction leaves no time for reflection, perspective, or time to elapse. What we say, think, and do most of the time in a reactive situation is not the proper choice. I'm guilty of using reaction as a self-defense mechanism. If people meet me with criticism, right or wrongly placed, I immediately jump to protect myself. I put on my, "No, I'm right" hat and run with it. Fortunately, with age, and the wisdom I've learned through time, even though I may experience the reactive phase of bad or threatening news initially, I now take a breath and assess the situation in hopes of a well-thought-out response.

I use the term *response* as the healthiest way to approach this subject. Allow me to use a basketball example. This react/response situation, unfortunately, has infiltrated our game to the point of embarrassment. I'm not talking about NBA players responding to adversity on the floor, but the fourth grade kid who can't accept a foul called on him. Really? What happened to our game? The next time you watch a game, pay attention to the reactions by players who are called for a foul, traveling, or any violation. With the whole world watching, the player can decide to respond or react. A reaction is usually an immediate, "Who, me?" or "I didn't touch him ref" and is accompanied by the arm and body gestures of a child. I consider myself an old-school purist when it comes to the great game of basketball. I abhor any player who disrespects the game by trying to save face when he's wrong. It signals a total lack of responsibility on a big stage where many young people are closely watching. "What's okay for an NBA idol is good enough for me," an 11-year-old may say. Some coaches, no matter the level, don't seem to care if their players act like spoiled brats or not. I do!

Every coach I ever played for made it clear that there would be no adverse reaction to any situation on the floor. In fact, some of them would take a player out of the game if he even looked in the vicinity of the official making the call. I've witnessed this many times and I have so much respect for this philosophy. My hope for the game is that every youth, junior high, high school, and professional coach would take this approach. It's Pollyanna thinking for sure, but it would be a great step to take to help save the sanctity of the game.

The most absurd element of this negative reaction is the fact that decisions on fouls are not likely to be overturned. About 99% of the time, the call will stand. Young players will consider the whistle and the foul call as a personal attack, knowing full well the call will never be reversed. In my Tough U basketball academy, I talk at great lengths to players about the adverse effects of bad body language. I ask, "What do you expect the ref to do, stop the game five minutes later and say he wants to overturn the call because #32 was crying about how it wasn't a foul?" Grow up and give me a break! Sports can expose the weaknesses of us all. Keep an eye on this fouling example and I'm sure you will be as shocked as well.

In chapter two, I explained about the absence of immunity when it comes to adversity. It's an unpleasant fact and will never change. We do have a choice in the decisions we make in the face of life's punches. Let's assume we can agree on the difference between reacting and responding. I'd like to challenge you to adopt a stance of response in life's challenging situations. When you do, the quality of your decisions will be greatly enhanced.

> *"A warrior takes his lot whatever it may be*
> *and accepts it in ultimate humbleness."*
> **~ Carlos Castaneda**

When you are faced with reacting to a positive or negative situation that looms in front of you, you have an opportunity to make a big decision that will affect your life one way or another. The right choices can strengthen your ability to respond to life, whereas poor decisions can start a snowball effect for all decisions to come. Making poor decisions is a slippery slope that you do not want to travel. I've been there, and trust me when I say it's like climbing a 15-foot ladder without steps. I hope this book, seen through my life's eye, will give you a reason to evaluate the health of your decisions in times of desperation and tragedy. If it does, every ounce of effort to write this book will be worth it many times over to me and to the people you love.

My journey illustrates the devastation of poor choices followed by unwise responses. You face life-defining consequences when these two are in tandem. Both can be part of the ugly reality of life on the run.

Don't run, please don't run.

Take a step back, put others first, and make the wisest decision possible at that exact point in time. As you consult with others, you will realize that your fight or flight way of doing things is flawed! You owe it to yourself and all others involved to be wise in times of difficulty.

Since we all know life will throw some knockout punches our way, it's best to expect them to come even though we might not know when they will rear their ugly heads. A fantastic example originates from a college basketball coach and friend, Tim Floyd.

Floyd had a very successful run at Iowa State from 1994-1998. His teams were stingy on defense and opportunistic on offense. He led his team to the Sweet Sixteen in 1996, losing to UCLA. In the summer of 1999 he was presented with the head coaching job of the legendary Chicago Bulls. His friend, Larry Eustachy, successful in his own right at Idaho and Utah State, became the new Cyclones coach. I was fortunate enough, due to my relationship with Tim, to join the new staff in Ames.

If memory serves me right, the world-ending issue in the office on that September morning of 2002 had to do with a player and academics. Imagine that!

Working for Eustachy was a rollercoaster. This particular morning though he was really wound tight. Floyd happened to be back in Ames and stopped by the office. He stood back and observed; a skill at which he is very astute. He said little, then added, "So did you think something like this wasn't going to happen?" followed by a chuckle. The banter went back and forth among staff members with Floyd setting up for the kill.

"Listen you guys, make it easy on yourselves, at the start of each season, make a list. List all the things that could happen to your players, coaches, and program. It will be a long list but that's just a fact. Now, when one of the things happens, just pick up the list and cross it off." The famous TF Adversity Checklist was born that day!

Floyd's admonition speaks to how we react quickly to anything that doesn't go as planned. We could all gain from adopting the TF Adversity Checklist philosophy. No, we don't encourage pain in our lives, but we do know it's coming. Take a deep breath, sit down, grab the list, and then make a plan to handle the situation.

> *"Life is like a grindstone, whether it wears you out or shines you up depends on what you are made of."*
>
> **~ Anonymous**

So, how do we handle things when they come? Let me share some basketball teaching with you to help. Basketball is a physical game where contact is the norm each time down the floor. Players are taught to accept the fact that contact, whether they like it or not, is a big factor against tougher, better teams.

**When teaching players how to best deal with contact, I share three rules:**

1.      **Expect contact.** Never be surprised by contact at any time. It's going to be there – so add it to the list and accept it.

2.      **When confronted with contact, don't back down.** You can choose to go around the body that's in your way, but by doing that you have made your shot attempt much more challenging than it needs to be. Identify the contact, and play through it as the aggressor. Play right through arms, elbows, and bodies on the way to the rim and you will minimize the contact substantially.

3.      **Keep your eyes on the rim.** This skill can make or break your ability to score. The flinch reaction forces us to squint or close our eyes just as we are about to get clobbered. It will hurt a lot less because of rule #1, I promise. Keeping your eyes on the rim is the last element of playing successfully against contact.

------

I recommend that we face adversity in an identical manner. Expect it, play through it, and keep your eyes open and then make the shot! You now have a chance to win the "game" in which you are so competitively involved.

# Chapter Four
# Rebound Forward, Maybe

*"Between stimulus and response, there is a space. In that space is our power to choose our response. In our response lies our growth and our freedom."*
**~ Viktor Frankl, Holocaust survivor**

We must decide what our choices are in the face of a life-defining moment. Our options include 1) doing nothing, 2) take the path of least resistance, avoid pain and responsibility, and turn to unhealthy choices or 3) turn adversity into an asset. Ask yourself, "Of all the bad things that have happened in my life, which course have I taken to get through to the other side in good shape?" Moving beyond difficulty and defeat takes patience, time, and resolve. It involves hard work and cannot be taken for granted.

If your response falls under the first option, you have looked at adversity, sat on it and done nothing. I don't recommend this for anyone. These people live in a state of numbness and say things like, "Nothing good ever happens to me," "Life sucks, and then you die," "I never win anything," and "I'd complain, but nobody would listen." They lose before the game ever begins. They create a "no win" attitude and convince themselves that trying to make a difference in life is useless. They fall short of their God-given opportunities and simply decide to stay on life's couch.

Kirk Ferentz is probably the best example of not lounging on life's couch. At the conclusion of the 2015-2016 season, Iowa football coach, Kirk Ferentz was asked how he would move forward. "If you have a tough year or tough ending like we did last year, you can respond to it or get in the fetal position and let people run you over." Thankfully, the

Hawkeye head man chose the right route in moving forward. I urge you to choose the right route to move your life forward.

> *"Some people really think they can avoid adversity. Trying to avoid adversity is like trying to avoid life."*
>
> ~ **Steve Kerr,**
> **Head Coach Golden State Warriors**

The second option deals with people who are worn down by things not working out or they are afraid to face reality. These people often live in fear of the next thunderbolt of life. Who doesn't want to avoid pain, right? But adversity throws our lives up for grabs and many times we have no idea how to handle it. I've always wondered how people without families and support survive. We all have an "I quit, this is too tough," reaction, but many rise above those initial feelings. When adversity and grief stack up, it was easier to give up.

The desire for comfort from pain causes us to avoid making decisions that require tremendous effort and patience. Taking this route may seem safe but it can lead to awful consequences.

Some of the things that can grow out of following this path are feelings of bitterness, reclusiveness, grief, abandonment, change in outlook on life, hopelessness, loss of purpose, failure, avoiding family, lack of financial contribution, poor health, anger, escapism, increased alcohol consumption, complaining 24/7, and trying to control everything. Other consequences include loss of pride in physical appearance, weight loss or weight gain, lack of faith, self-pity, distorted perspective, holding onto the past, no forward vision, lack of acceptance, divorce, depression, self-soothing at any cost, recklessness, lack of wisdom, keeping it all in without sharing with anyone, prison, and for some, suicidal thoughts.

The hope for us all is to take on a face-to-face challenge with confidence. The people who choose option three most often make healthy choices on how to navigate the long road to a desirable conclusion. They lean on others to guide and support them. They can clearly sense the other side of the bridge even when it's not in sight. Because of their past efforts and plans, they know this obstacle will fortify them and make them stronger and more able to handle the next rough patch.

We've all heard it said, "It's not what happens to you, it's how you respond." Also, "When you get knocked down, you have to get right back up." These are encouraging statements, but not all of us respond the same way. Basketball helps illustrate this point.

One of our tenets of toughness during our championship era at Iowa State was playing through injury. When knocked to the floor during a game, our players were subject to the three-second rule, which stated that players have three seconds to get to their feet. If they did, they stayed in the game and if not, we substituted for them.

The idea comes from building a mental toughness persona to intimidate the opponent. Imagine the thoughts of our opponent as one of our players is knocked hard to the floor by taking an offensive charge and is clearly in great pain. The injured player pops up and prepares for the next play. The key was staying in the game, and our players had an amazing ability to pop up. They not only sprang back up, but they rebounded forward by their resilience!

The wise way to live often results from being uncomfortable in the process of struggle. Many people run from difficulty or try to find ways to experience comfort in the midst of pain. An ideal choice often comes by making an uncomfortable decision. People who do this see the finish line and know that positive results come from incredible effort and patience.

Let's return to the elderly man's journey through his neighborhood. Fortunately, he found a bright side to adversity in numerous homes; many spoke *only* of the strength they gained after being knocked down. The man was so encouraged he began to look at hardship in a whole new light. The people who faced adversity with determination gained a better perspective, became stronger mentally, spiritually, and physically, experienced positive life changes, increased faith in God, gained clarity, developed laser vision, experienced deeper relationships, focused purpose, and were more likely to enjoy outdoor activities, exercise, hobbies, and socializing. They had a game plan for the rest of life. They had a choice.

The choice is to become better, not bitter. But I warn you that once you make a decision, it only holds as long as you stay committed to it. Our emotions tug at us constantly, and moving past adversity to become better may be fleeting. Of course, the opposite can be true, too.

After some research, I found that the topic of adversity seems to be misrepresented. Almost every resource, mainly books, approach adversity with a positive, uplifting spin. Because there is an opportunity for good to come from difficult situations, it doesn't mean that the world becomes wonderful every time. I just don't see it that way. Dealing with adversity is hard work and can ravage you and slam you to the mat.

You need to understand that the result of adversity can lead to death, loss, addiction, prison, bankruptcy, isolation and more. Very few want to portray this downturn in their lives. The positive feels better and maybe that's why descriptions of adversity are "a friend," "a blessing," "upside," "a gift," "welcome," "triumph," "joy," an "advantage," or "magic." When I read *"Steps to Overcome Life Crisis,"* I immediately thought, "What if they don't" What now? — *Plan?*

My hope is that everyone can triumph over adversity, but history shows this is just not the case. This is a soft approach to something we must all take very seriously. It may look good on the bestseller display, but it doesn't come that easy or at all.

Not everyone makes appropriate decisions in the throes of difficulty. Some are prepared for the onslaught of adversity while others are mowed down in its path. Many factors come into play once the bad news arrives in our lives. It's what we do next that makes all the difference.

The first challenge is to acknowledge the tragedy has hit home. Some stop in their tracks immediately. Most are shocked, angry, numb, or dismissive initially. *Time is not a quick fix but a slow healer.* I remember after losing our girls, which I'll talk more about in Chapters Eight and Nine, someone told me that the death of a child is like an open wound. I felt like that statement was so true...when Meredith and Natalie left us, it felt as if a deep gash had injured my arm and it was bleeding profusely. I was in physical and emotional shock, not knowing if I would live or die.

> **"Pain is inevitable; suffering is optional."**
> **~ Unknown**

Even a deep wound begins to heal once it's been properly tended to, although the process is extremely painful. Sometimes infection sets in, and the body part feels the effects of the injury. My soul felt the pain and the festering of infection when day after day I attempted to heal from this loss...this wound. Deep wounds look ugly, but ever so slowly they begin to heal. Often the wound rubs against an object or is bumped, causing immediate sharp pain and memories of the injury. I would smell a scent, see a photo, or hear a song and it was like crashing my heart wound into a wall. The pain lingers for a time and then subsides over time. With a physical injury, fresh bandages are placed strategically and ever so carefully, and as the skin tissue heals around the wound, the gash is eventually not as gruesome as it was initially but can still be painful to the touch. While a wounded heart is healing, you can't see the tears, but you can feel the tenderness when a sudden memory floods in like a torrent. The soul still experiences pain during the healing process while new hope is birthed and healing is taking place in the hidden recesses.

Some days the wound is out of sight and out of mind. Other days its memory lingers like a dark shadow that follows me everywhere. Those are difficult days. The shadow of each dark day is followed by a softer, lighter one. Then, for some reason, they stack up like dominoes and the cumulative effect can become unbearable. Finally, years down the road, a physical wound is replaced by a scar. The physical pain subsides, but the scar serves forever as a reminder of the injury. That pain will never go away but time has done its job. The same thing happens with a wounded heart – a scar serves forever as a reminder of what once was. Our little girls will always live in my heart, inside the scar that now stands as a memorial of their precious lives.

The challenge for us all is to handle tough times appropriately. Being the poster child for escaping pain through avoidance, I can tell you it does nothing but add to the burden. This approach has left me with permanent residual physical, emotional, and psychological damage. Please listen as I beg you not to take my path. As I read once, it's like being chained to a dead man. I drug one around far too long.

"Avoidance"

# Chapter Five
# The Old Oak Tree

*"Amidst the confusion of the times, the conflicts of conscience, and the turmoil of daily living, an abiding faith becomes an anchor to our lives."*

**~ Thomas S. Monson**

My childhood is jam-packed with vivid memories of fishing. More than any other activity, fishing was a way for my brothers and me to spend time together with our dad. As a sports and outdoor editor for 37 years, he bestowed us with his presence and thousands of hours of casting and netting fish. My formative years were filled with dozens of trips to Canada and Minnesota. Loaded to the gills with equipment, we eagerly jumped into the boat every morning, facing yet another action-packed day.

Sixteen-hour days were more common than not. Always part of the necessary equipment was an anchor. If not trolling or casting shorelines and docks, we would find a spot and anchor. It allowed us to get set and familiar with a specific radius of water and lake structure. My dad was a seasoned fisherman and he'd use this strategy to hone in on fish who were grouped in a particular area. It's all part of the thrill of the hunt.

Anchoring your boat is a lot like having a base in your life. It provides a place you can go to step back and analyze events of the day. Taking a careful look at past choices and considering those you will make in the future will allow for right decision-making. When the lake or sea of your life is rough, you can always "anchor" yourself to return to the values and core beliefs that are truly yours.

Hmmm?? I'm lost ☹

Anchors in your life take many forms. Some find that people or material things serve this function, and others find it with self-destructive behavior and isolation. Drinking, drugs, pornography, sex, and gambling suck in a large number of men who are troubled. Men with strong convictions turn instantly to their faith for counsel, comfort, and insight. Some melt at the challenge while others seem indifferent and do nothing.

I challenge you to look inward and discover the truths about your anchor in the deep waters of life's tough times. To achieve a healthy conclusion, it's critical that you have a consistent ability to deal with pain and trials that arise. The key lies in which anchor you choose to guide you to safety and sanity.

Some people we encounter in life we are meant to meet. There is a flow to our exchanges, smiles and glances. We experience this oneness very rarely in our lives. When I entered prison at Butner Federal Correctional Institution, I convinced myself that the differences between others and me far outweighed the commonalities. After a few months, as I stood in the common area up front, I heard someone say, "Hey, that's Ced; Ced's back."

Watching from a distance, I could tell that Cedric Barnes was a special person. I learned later that he had survived double bypass heart surgery the previous week; yet this was only a chapter in the incredible book on Cedric Barnes. I shook his hand and introduced myself briefly, feeling an urge to know this man in a much deeper way.

A week later, I was sitting up front reading, *Muhammad Ali: His Life and Times.* Cedric slowly walked by me, doing a double take at seeing my reading choice. He turned around and stared at the book cover as I read. Slowly, he shook his head and said, "Beautiful book, beautiful book." As they say, the rest is history. Cedric entered my life at the perfect moment and will never leave it. He is a man of remarkable character traits. As a promising athlete, he lacked guidance and fell to the evils of the world. Instead of the NBA, prison was calling his name. For 23 years he toiled behind bars in unthinkable environments. I've told him that no more than one man in a hundred could have withstood the pressures and dangers of forced animalistic survival, and he is such a man.

> **"When we long for life without difficulties, remind us that oaks grow strong in contrary winds and diamonds are made under pressure."**
>
> **~ Peter Marshall**

Ced left an indelible mark on my life. A friend forever, I will always remember him as a man of dignity, respect, perseverance, compassion, perspective, and warmness. He taught me great lessons on humility and the value of living each day at a time. I promised Ced that one day we would sit at Tiger Stadium together as giddy as two kids playing hooky from school. Friends forever.

After serving 23 years in prison, Ced was released two months before I was. I had a tough time fathoming that he wouldn't be part of my daily life at Butner. I was crying like a child as I walked with him to the processing center for his release. I was torn up on two fronts. First, I was afraid for him because he entered prison while Michael Jordan was still in college. Would he be able to adjust to the world he left so long ago? But I also grieved because my heart left with Ced that day. He meant so much to me. As sturdy as a two-by-four, Ced reminded me, "Don't cry because you have to say goodbye; ~TTU, smile because it happened." – coaching BBS, NHS, BHS, TMS, FHS, KC

Ced quoted a passage from a devotional book by Charles E. Cowman and Jim Reimann, called *Streams in the Desert: 366 Daily Devotional Readings[1]*, "You are the tree planted where the fierce winds twist its branches and bend its trunk—often

---

[1] http://www.zondervan.com/streams-in-the-desert-4

nearly to the point of breaking. The strongest and greatest character is grown through hardship."

**"God does not want us to be like greenhouse plants, which are sheltered from rough weather, but like storm-beaten oaks. These are the trees that toolmakers seek for handles for their tools, because of their great strength."**

**~ L.B. Cowman**

The oak tree refuses to let the world shape it; it relies on experience, knowledge, and solid footing. The oak tree makes decisions based on truth and experience because at its core is a firm foundation. When a decision lies in front of you, your foundation can make all the difference. Is it built on sand or stone? A stone foundation helps you stay grounded. When a big windstorm hits, a house built on sand is gone in an instant as is everything in it. Stand firm in your convictions.

How deeply are you rooted? Study a picture of the oak tree to realize the root system is much bigger and more intricately designed than the above ground tree. The foundation of roots holds it in place while the trunk and leaves give it its beauty. What you see is admired, and what you don't see allows it to be admired! My friend Cedric lives a life grounded with a root system ten hurricanes couldn't move. He is the old oak tree to me!

## Chapter Six
## Nugent, Nightcrawlers, and KAAY

*"Cure for an obsession; get another one."*
*~ Mason Cooley*

John D. Rockefeller, an Ohio native, started Standard Oil. He was at one point the world's richest man and first-ever American billionaire. When asked, "How much money is enough," he responded, "Just a little bit more."

My past was about being highly organized and driven, constantly going all out, making sure the job was done right, and at times, I was reckless in my pursuit. I would do anything to accomplish the end goal. At an early age, I understood that achievement was important and success started by giving yourself every possible chance to be the best. I was destined to be a multitasker to the nth degree. It was the rush I was looking for and that came in many forms: alcohol, pornography, movies, concerts, memorabilia, basketball and baseball cards, networking, overworking, career building, film breakdown, scouting reports, recruiting, winning, striving to be the best, golf, fishing, Diet Coke, Iowa Hawkeye football, concerts, and very loud music. In fishing vernacular, there's no such thing as "the last cast," as long as you have "one more cast."

*"Earth provides enough to satisfy every man's needs but not every man's greed."*
**~ Mahatma Gandhi**

In life, I've experienced success, sense of purpose, fulfillment, and accomplishment. Did it come at a cost? The original game plan didn't include a long list of losses. I am so grateful to have had a chance to coach at the highest collegiate level. The experiences and people I've met along the way can never be replaced. In reflection, I do wonder at the price I paid to win the next game or recruit the hottest new prospect. I know that I gave the game my best, starting every day cocked, locked and ready to rock, Doc! I play with that same intensity when it comes to my music collection.

Owning a thousand albums was never the goal. It started with a couple and then two dozen. Then I added 8-tracks and cassettes. When CDs hit the scene, I wondered where the music format world would end. There was talk of the L-Cassette and other new inventions. For me, collecting never stopped regardless of the audio format. Once I got hooked, it was over. I wanted anything that was foot stompin', blood pumping and guitar-driven. I was fascinated with the different approaches to music and leaned early toward the loud and raw variety. That has yet to stop! Today I don't have a thousand albums, just 310, as well as 2,000 CDs, two Daisy Dillman Band 8-tracks along with a handful of rare 45s.

**"Obsession is the single most wasteful human activity, because with an obsession you keep coming back and back and back to the same question and never get an answer."**
**~ Norman Mailer**

Never having quite enough is a plight. Fear of missing out or "FOMO" is "a pervasive apprehension that others might be having rewarding experiences from which one is absent." This social angst is characterized by "a desire to stay continually connected with what others are doing." FOMO is also defined as "a fear of regret" which may lead to a compulsive concern that one might miss an opportunity for social interaction, a novel experience, profitable investment or other satisfying events. In other words, FOMO perpetuates the fear of having made the wrong decision on how to spend time, as "You can imagine how things could be different."

It becomes the chase, a game. The music is an afterthought. I'm a sucker for new music as if the sound, instruments or ripping guitars will be something totally different from what I've heard so far. I love the history of music as much as anything, and concerts have always been a fascination of mine. The Crossroads in Mississippi, the blues of Memphis, Sun Recording Studio, the Motley House in West Hollywood, Tina's Grocery in Milwaukee, The Rainbow, Lemmy's apartment, Ronnie Van Zandt's childhood home, Folsom and Muscle Shoals. Lunacy is having a personal music museum with in excess of one thousand artists represented. But like I said earlier, "A thousand albums were not the goal, but a thousand artists were."

Another full circle moment occurred on August 3, 2017 in Clear Lake, Iowa at the famous Surf Ballroom.

The history-rich Surf hosted the Winter Dance Party on February 2, 1959, which included Buddy Holly, J.P. "The Big Bopper" Richardson, Ritchie Valens, and Dion. It was the last show Holly, Richardson, and Valens would ever play as their plane crashed the next day, February 3rd, just miles from takeoff in a frozen Iowa cornfield near Clear Lake, headed to Fargo, North Dakota.

On this recent August night, Ted Nugent punished amplifiers and eardrums like never before. Performing his 6,613th concert, he led into the legendary song, "Fred Bear." He told a story about working jobs as a kid to earn money for a guitar and later, a bow and arrow. Ted's dad told Ted to get two jobs to pay for each. His bow and arrow were bought from money he earned by selling nightcrawlers. Because I first heard Stranglehold while hunting nightcrawlers, it became another full circle moment thanks to Rock n' Roll.

**Nugent**

These words on the back of the new album in my hands bolted my Converse low cuts to the floor: "With knowing grins and clenched fists in the Midwest..." The photo on the cover of his debut effort, "Ted Nugent," drew me in like a magnet. He looked like half-man, half-creature. His hair was massive and unkept but it was his eyes that symbolized the relentless zeal for the hard-driving rock 'n' roll he played. I had heard of the Detroit guitarist from my brother Rick, who had mentioned the Amboy Dukes to me one day in our shared bedroom. I thought his name was Ted Nugget, not Nugent. I learned quickly that Ted headed up the Amboy Dukes out of Detroit. CREEM magazine became a monthly purchase to learn as much as I could about the world of rock n' roll.

In April 1968, *Journey to the Center of the Mind* hit the music world like a hurricane. The song still makes its way into commercials and movies. At the time, the Amboy Dukes were no different to me from the other bands that shared our single turntable. Albums from Rare Earth, Steppenwolf, CCR, Led Zeppelin, Chicago and Three Dog Night were frequently spun. Over time I could tell "Proud Mary" from "Celebrate." But it wasn't until I stumbled upon a radio station in Arkansas that my life adopted music as a full-time obsession. Nugent became real and I jumped on the bandwagon.

**Nightcrawlers**

"Walleyes love nightcrawlers." I remember seeing that slogan as a kid somewhere. This fact took us outside on rain-soaked nights in search of the biggest, fattest, juiciest crawlers we could get in a can. Preparing for our Canadian fishing trip was part of the fun for boat mate's brother Roger, and Bill and Terry Huseman. "If you're going to use them, you'll have to go get 'em," Dutch, the elder Huseman, told us in that unmistakable voice.

One clear June night we made a big haul. Rain provides nightcrawlers an opportunity to travel out of their holes to areas unavailable on dry ground - the hunter is required to creep slowly on his knees, armed with a coffee can and flashlight. Being very sensitive to light, these monsters were tricky to catch. To be less obvious, we covered the lens of our flashlight with red cellophane that reduced the intensity of the light. The poor worms were defenseless against us and we were able to pick them off two or three at a time. We learned to pinch the crawlers as near to their hole as possible and then carefully ease the rest of the body out. They had the uncanny knack of getting away and disappearing back home. With the going prices for "nighties" in Canada, we were earning our way to the Great White North by securing our quota of 75 dozen crawlers.

## KAAY

Spinning the dial in bed one night, I stumbled onto an underground rock station, KAAY, in Little Rock, Arkansas. The concept was known as album rock, a term unknown to me. It hooked me instantly as radio took on a whole new meaning; the music was nothing like I had ever heard. The main DJ was a mysterious man who went by the name of Clyde Clifford. He talked slowly and as little as possible. Spaced out sounds filled the long gaps between his thoughts. This music by the group Head was entitled Cannabis Sativa, I learned many years later. He loved to play long instrumentals, sometimes filling an hour with three or four songs. It was here that I first heard "Roundabout" by Yes, "In My Time of Dying" and "Stairway to Heaven" by Led Zeppelin, "Slow Ride" by Foghat, and anything by the Allman Brothers. We were listening to KAAY on our nightcrawler hunt that night. I had just spotted a mating session in progress through my red-filtered lens. We called that a double, which would earn you top status as a nightie hunter. After successfully pinching the mating pair of nightcrawlers at the base, I heard the sound of a cutting guitar begin a song known as "Stranglehold." Sitting on the stump of a nearby box elder tree, the radio delivered a song that would change me forever. No opening guitar riff will ever match it. I was frozen in place as rain poured down, capturing every note. Unfortunately, I had to wait through three other songs and 40 minutes to learn of the song's performer, Ted Nugent.

For about five bucks, I bought the album and it remains my most influential five-dollar purchase. The intrigue of the music opened a whole new world that I knew existed but had yet to taste. I assumed that rock performers made decent money, but something else had to drive this guy to play with such fury and vigor. To me, he represented a spirit of freedom and unbridled passion for his craft of hard-driving rock 'n' roll, each song played like it was his last show. The Nugent craze led me on a journey that to this day I'm amazed I pulled off. Stay with me here...I'm headed somewhere...

———

## Ted Nugent's New Year's Eve Whiplash Bash

For Christmas 1991, my family headed back to Iowa for the holidays. With a short window between pre- and post-Christmas games, 20 hours on the road didn't add up. Being on my own in Oxford, Ohio allowed for massive office time, video tape and recruiting work. An independent type, I relished the *it's ok!* time alone. Except for two days during Christmas, our team practiced. Upon checking out the practice schedule, a light went off. A morning practice on December 31 meant that I would have the rest of the day to myself. I checked the practice time for New Year's Day and it was set at 9:00 a.m. That left an entire day in between team practices. Ted Nugent's New Year's Eve Whiplash Bash took place every year in Detroit's Cobo Center. I had read about this unbridled display of energy, thumping bass guitar, and Ted screaming at the top of his lungs as the ball dropped on another year. That very second, I got excited about the prospect of going, I withdrew from the idea, knowing that our head coach was unpredictable at best and could change the practice times or else schedule a team meeting. Ultimately, though, I knew that in years to come I'd be glad I saddled up and took the trip to Detroit.

*Rebound Forward*

As was true with most road trips, to me the five-hour drive was nothing. Music blared as I ripped through Dayton, Lima, and Toledo before hitting Michigan. Ten hours on the road was a small price to pay for someone who loves rock 'n' roll. I parked on the roof of Joe Louis Arena, which sits next to Cobo, and walked through the Detroit car show on my way to the ticket office, paying no attention to the new car models. It was a ticket I wanted. Praying for general admission tickets, I got my wish. I wanted to be in the thick mass of humanity to view the insane antics of the Motor City Madman.

The show was beyond anything I had ever seen. After welcoming the New Year, he continued to play and play and play. At the conclusion of the concert, the Cobo floor was littered with *confetti* from the rafters and seasoned dried deer venison from the stage. Once the crowd began to leave, I scurried around on the floor to gather as many packages as possible. This was one of my "fear-of-missing-out" moments. I didn't want to leave but knew I had a lot of road ahead of me.

With my ears ringing, I was one of the last to leave the building. In amazement, I watched roadies tear down the stage, wishing I could join them. Heading south of Detroit, then through Toledo, the windows were down and the freezing cold January 1992 air ripped through my hair. It was a matter of staying awake now. I was forced to stop twice to sleep without an alarm clock. Each nap was quick but helped me to get back on the road. It would be a race to the finish as I begged to arrive at Millet Hall in time for practice. With luck, I reached the office at 8:40 a.m. and rushed onto the floor. Everything was as if I had never left Oxford almost a day earlier. The only difference was the sharp ringing in my ears. I did my best to stay out of the way that day, knowing I couldn't hear the player right next to me.

It was a trip for the ages. It also signaled what I call a "full circle" experience. I had no idea at the time that I would return to Cobo Hall in 14 weeks to compete in the MAC post-season basketball tournament. With wonder, I surveyed the upper decks of Cobo and showed our student managers exactly where I had stood for the Whiplash Bash. As usual, they returned nothing but head shakes and snickers. "You're crazy, RB!" In a 58-57 nail-biter, we downed a good Ball State team and advanced to the 1992 NCAA Tournament. I love Cobo Hall!

Years later in 1999, I met my rock hero, Ted Nugent, after a concert with Kiss and Skid Row in a locker room in Hilton Coliseum. A moment I had rehearsed a million times became a reality. A concealed mini tape recorder captured the encounter. As a 44-year-old who is used to performing in front of thousands of people, I was close to speechless. After revealing to Ted that I had seen him 20 times, he informed me that I had attitude. It would be like Mozart saying your musical genius was beyond comprehension. Ted said that I had attitude. My current total for attending Ted's concerts stands at 25, and I'm hoping to soon top the 30 plateaux. As much as the album set me off, a live performance is impossible to describe. For some it's chefs, politicians, racecar drivers, shortstops, or scientists that draw them in. For me, it was Ted Nugent who set the standard for passion, drive, and commitment.

"Uncle Ted" gave me the kick start I needed for the obsession and drive that has ignited me in my professional and personal life. Those who know me would say that I've accomplished things based on laser focus, preparation, and a relentless effort — just as Nuge did before me.

The only person to rival my loyalty to Ted Nugent came at age 13 when I heard of a basketball player who was scoring 40 and 50 points a game. *No way that's possible*, I thought. Sure enough, there was a young basketball player in Louisiana taking the hoop world by storm. Pistol Pete Maravich hit the scene at Louisiana State University in Baton Rouge as a freshman during the 1966-67 season, averaging a staggering 43.6 points per game. The NCAA prohibited freshmen from playing varsity ball at the time so he went berserk in 19 freshman tilts. The freshman team often drew more than twice as many fans to its games as the struggling varsity did. By the way, the Tigers' head coach was none other than the "Pistol Pete's" father, Press Maravich.

## Maravich Mania

I sat on the edge of my bed, thinking how it was possible to average 44 points per game. In my church league and youth games, I scored 12 points and was the team's high scorer. Our team total may have reached 30. I was instantly swept up in Maravich mania. I wanted to know everything about the Pistol. I researched his background and previous scoring averages and found out he started for his high school varsity in eighth grade, which was an unheard-of feat. He was a small, frail youngster but tougher than most. He spent every waking moment in the gym. He dribbled to and from school. His dad took him out for drives where Pete would dribble out the window. He was legendary for attending the movies, dribbling with his right hand on the right aisle, then moving to the left hand at intermission.

No one in the world was as obsessed toward a single goal as Pete. My love for the game made it a natural for me to get in line. Basketball was and would forever be an obsession to me. I practiced for eight hours a day, broken into three segments. I shot and shot and shot. I mimicked Pete's moves, shots, and behind-the-back dribble. Limited by gravity and slow feet, I made up for it with passion, heart, and pure love for the game. School notebooks were littered with names of players, teams and, of course, tons of Maravich references.

## The Son of a Sportswriter            hmmm? / Alaska,

My greatest memory with my dad was when I was 15-years-old and we took a basketball trip together in the winter of 1972. The trip would triangle between Fort Dodge, Iowa, Lawrence, Kansas, and Kansas City, Missouri. Being the son of a sportswriter had its privileges for sure. On Saturday night, we saw the Iowa Hawkeyes beat the Kansas Jayhawks in famed Phog Allen Fieldhouse. We loitered in the Hawkeyes' locker room after the game, and star guard Rick Williams presented me with his sweaty socks. I stuffed them in my coat pocket as my dad interviewed the winning coach, Dick Schultz. Little did I know I would return to this legendary building 28 years later. This time, instead of being in a front row seat, I had a bench seat as an assistant coach for Iowa State. I remember the seat I sat in as a 15-year-old being directly behind the bench. It was another amazing full circle moment.

We left Sunday morning for Kansas City. We made the lobby of the Muehlebach Hotel our afternoon headquarters. As far as I knew at the time it was just another downtown hotel, but I would later learn the Muehlebach had welcomed celebrities including Helen Keller, Ernest Hemingway, Babe Ruth, Frank Sinatra, Bob Hope, Elvis Presley, and The Beatles. The hotel also hosted Presidents Theodore Roosevelt, Woodrow Wilson, Calvin Coolidge and Herbert Hoover, and Missouri-native Harry S. Truman stayed in the Presidential Suite so frequently that the Muehlebach became known as White House West.

We camped in the lobby until I spotted a member of the Hawks' team, Walt Bellamy, and then saw Herm Gilliam followed by "Sweet" Lou Hudson.

My heart jumped in anticipation of the superstar that covered the walls of my room with over 300 pictures and posters. Finally, I uttered, "There he is!" I was in shock and unable to move from my chair as I gawked at Pistol Pete Maravich in the flesh. He looked eight foot tall. My dad nudged me to get up and talk to him but I wanted no part of it. Finally, after signing a few autographs, he moved toward the elevator. A group of senior class Ames High School players were already there. Ironically, later I would become dear friends with Steve Burgason, one of those waiting. Before it was too late, I took off and joined the group outside the elevator.

Maravich greeted us and invited us up to his hotel room. Frozen, I slightly nodded in agreement. Trying not to stare at him as we ascended to the fifth floor, I was convinced my mom would be waking me for school any second. We followed him to his room and sat on the corner of the bed. I salivated as I noticed two pairs of Pro-Keds gray suede low cuts strewn on the floor. Small talk about our teams began as the Little Cyclone players talked about their #1 ranked team in Iowa, and I hoped he wouldn't ask about me. He didn't. After what seemed like two hours, he thanked us for coming and said he needed a little sleep before the game. He shook my hand on the way out. I pledged that I'd never wash it and followed the older guys to the down elevator.

My dad wanted every detail, play by play, as we went to eat. The half-pound of wintergreen mints I downed while nervously waiting for Maravich sat like an anchor in my stomach, but we ordered pizza anyway. My dad described our dinner as "a meal he chose but never tasted."

The rest of the day and night was a blur. Although Pete threw in 37 two nights earlier against the Washington Bullets, he struggled to a 17-point outing as the Kings defeated the Hawks, 130-115. We witnessed a historical effort by Lou Hudson who scored 43 points, while the King's Nate Archibald banged in 41. It was during this 1972-73 season that Archibald led the NBA in scoring (34.0) and assists (11.4). As amazing as those performances were, my focus was on Maravich. Post-game security had not yet arrived in the NBA in 1972, so we were allowed into the inner sanctums of old Kansas City Auditorium. We waited outside the Hawks' locker room with others. Reminiscent of Beatle hysteria, throngs of girls could be heard screaming for the Pistol just down the hall.

The door opened and reporters were shuffled into the musty, close quarters of the Hawks' locker room. My dad began to speak to Hawks' Coach Cotton Fitzsimmons and his players. I stood two inches from Lou Hudson's rusty PE locker as he walked out of the shower and excused himself. In awe, I noticed players were drinking beer, laughing, and toweling off. We waited anxiously for Pete, one of the last players to leave. My dad thanked Pete for the greatest basketball memory a young man could ever dream of. Pete looked at me and shook my hand as we stepped into the hallway. To avoid the onslaught of fans, he said, "Let's go this way," and signaled that we leave by a door that led to the sidewalk on the East side of the auditorium. Pete led me next to him as we walked up the hill to the Muehlebach. Walking slowly, he apologized to me for not playing well. He said it was tough as a young player in the NBA with all the games, but he would practice his shooting before the next game. Before I knew it, we stood at the entrance of the hotel's door. He said, "Goodbye, Randy, and remember what I said up in the room. <u>Practice every day, because if you don't, somebody is, and when you meet he will win!</u>"

Pete Maravich's advice would serve as the mantra for my life. Never, never let up or someone else will pass you by. Professionally and personally, my life would never leave those tracks rushing forward at maximum speed. Wise use of timeless advice? Absolutely!

# Chapter Seven
## You're Hired, You're Fired, You're History

*"I was always a kid that was afraid he was missing something."*
~ **Stevie Ray Vaughan**

At age 20, the thought of becoming a college basketball coach was daunting. But once I learned that college coaches don't teach class, instead they do "basketball stuff" all day, I knew it had to happen. *And* they pay you for it!

I was somewhat blinded by my exuberance for this career. I talked with several people about following this path, and although they encouraged me to pursue the college level, I knew that none of them actually gave me much of a chance of making it a reality. But I wasn't going to let others' lack of enthusiasm stop me. On the spot, I made three goals for my career:

1. Become a Division I college basketball assistant.
2. Become a Division I Head Coach.
3. Coach in the NCAA Final Four.

Thanks to a few late-game plays by eventual National Champion Michigan State in 2000, I fell short of my third goal.

Being the son of a sports writer, I spent many nights as a youth in gyms, soaking up the coaches, players, and the atmosphere. It was readily apparent to me that I belonged on the sideline. High school coaching was the logical starting point for me since experience is irreplaceable. As a college junior at the University of Iowa, I learned that a local high school, Iowa City Regina, needed a JV and varsity assistant boys coach.

Once I landed that first job, I never looked at academics the same way again. They became a means to an end. Sometimes I think about what I actually got my Master's Degree in at the University of Arizona. I truly don't remember going to class but must have because I earned my degree in Educational Administration.

The next two career stops were at West Branch High School a few miles outside of Iowa City where I did my student teaching and coaching. After a semester, I returned to the U of I to get certified to teach math at Pleasant Valley High School in the Quad Cities. The job was in the bank, but a full semester of math courses and teaching methods were required first. It's amazing what you can do when your back is to the wall. My three-year employment as coach and teacher at Pleasant Valley ended when I got the call from Scott Thompson of the University of Arizona.

Scott informed me I had been selected as the next graduate assistant in Tucson under Hall of Fame Coach Lute Olson, who had taken his Iowa team to the 1980 Final Four while I was a student. I had religiously attended practice to learn Olson's ways, and it is the foundation I stand on today. To work for Lute was a dream I never could have created, but it came true. I learned more from Lute in two seasons than I ever thought possible. His first-class approach and ability to manage a high-major program, as well as bring in the country's best players, was his genius. Lute was a shrewd tactician and his game adjustments were the best in the profession. Lute is retired and living in Tucson. He is a member of the Naismith Basketball Hall of Fame. I owe everything to Coach Olson for giving me the opportunity to be a college coach.

The Arizona experience offered me a learning opportunity like none other. Lute was known to hire great assistant coaches and the group at Arizona was the best. All future college head coaches, I worked daily with Ken Burmeister, Scott Thompson, Ricky Byrdsong, and Kevin O'Neill. Burmeister would lead programs at University of

Texas-San Antonio, Loyola-Chicago, and Incarnate Word. Thompson, a former Iowa Hawkeye guard, became the head man at Rice, Wichita State, and Cornell. Byrdsong and O'Neill would both coach at Northwestern in the Big 10. Byrdsong, tragically gunned down in a hate crime spree after his coaching career, was also the head man at Detroit-Mercy. O'Neill rose quickly, becoming the head coach at Marquette, Tennessee, Northwestern, and assistant coach with the New York Knicks, Indiana Pacers, Detroit Pistons, Memphis Grizzlies, and Toronto Raptors. He also served as head coach of the Toronto Raptors for one year.

My constant companion for two years was a graduate assistant also, Tom Billeter. Tom matriculated at the University of Illinois and had been on campus a year prior to my arrival. He and his wife Paula were on the same basketball journey as Mary Jo and I. We were driven, worked hard, spent crazy hours in the office, and were always thirsty. We spent hours in Tom and Paula's tiny one-bedroom apartment, drinking leftover beer from booster functions. Somehow, we always ordered more than we actually needed! We gazed down on the Bashful Bandit bar and wondered how long we would last in that place. These were great times for two young couples with stars in their eyes concerning the college coaching profession. We ran camps, picked up Lute's laundry, checked classes, rebounded shots for Sean Elliott and Steve Kerr at night, and any duty reserved for teeth-cutting graduate assistants. We cut and edited video tape on two video machines. An 18-inch stick was painted light blue and was used to tap start, stop and edit buttons from at least a few feet from the screen. The color selection was a stab at the University of North Carolina's famous color scheme. Certainly, the Heels aren't controlling their VCR's with painted rulers.

Lute switched us up on road trips; Tom making the Washington/Washington State trip as I would take Oregon/ Oregon State. Every second was a thrill as I thought back on teaching high school math and coaching JV hoops. We were so inspired we even ran the campus on beautiful fall mornings.

Leaving Bob Dobb's after "Monday Night Club," Tom would say, "See you in a few hours." Sure enough, we bounced back and answered the bell as we could easily do at that age. Monday Night Club was our opportunity to meet up after our evening graduate class and review our notes. Somehow, it took four hours to get through the notes. At Bob Dobb's the bar was extremely useful when Tom would bring his 6-month-old son, Michael, with him on Saturday afternoons. Many a time Tom changed "June Bug" right there on the bar. Adding to an amazing opportunity was the presence of another Iowan, Steve Condon. Condo was always in the middle of the action and ready for a Barney Fife quote, a joke, or a story, "You had probably never heard." A jack-of-all-trades, Condo was an excellent trainer and as you waited for a player to arrive at practice, Condo's training room was the first place I checked. He even fixed Tom J "Toody" Cirincione's black thick-rimmed glasses at basketball camp one hot July day. Toody, a legendary figure in the summer basketball camp circuit uttered, "Condo, you're a mechanical genius." Never a dull moment working for the Wildcats, providing life long memories, friends, and laughter.

My two-year GA position at the University of Arizona finished in the summer of 1987. Sure, I had been spoiled with starting out in a big-time program, first class travel and accommodations, Pac-10 Championships, NCAA Tournaments, and a chance to coach future NBA Champions Steve Kerr, Sean Elliot, and Jud Buechler. But it was time to move on and I accepted an assistant coaching job working for Gary Garner at Drake University. I quickly learned that I was working for a real "ball coach" and had to be on my toes every day. With a back seat littered with yellow legal pads, Garner was the consummate strategist. "Randy, reach back there and grab one of those pads" was a warning that a motion offense that couldn't be defended was on the way. He was a master at knowing the answer, then asking you a question to see how you would respond. I learned the hard way and it prepared me for all future encounters.

The most impactful question Gary asked me was within the first month of being on the Bulldog staff. He was curious about my philosophy of the game and asked, "Are you an offensive or defensive coach, Randy?" Like most cocky 30-year-olds would spout, "I think I'm pretty good at both of them." In an instant, you could hear the teeth of the bear trap snapping shut. He baited me into a conversation headed in the direction he planned. The question is one I talk about today with coaches because it is the most crucial decision one can make as a coach. Gary said you have to choose one end of the floor, either the defensive or offensive end first. Then choose the top three things that you most believe in and want your team to stand for. I quickly learned that Garner's foundation started and ended with great, fundamental defense.

That memorable day I officially became a defensive coach first, then was introduced to the concept of defensive transition known as 'Get Back'. It is the greatest lesson I've ever learned as a coach and I owe Gary for that. An amazing 13-5 season turned into 14-14, as we lost nine of our last ten. A laundry list of odd finishes and phantom calls doomed us. It was a real kick in the teeth when Garner was unjustly fired as head coach at the end of the season. You could see the brilliance of Garner as Drake's coach but the decision-makers were blind. The finality of getting fired was gut wrenching. Fellow assistant Terry Carroll and I drove aimlessly around Des Moines without a clue as to what we would do next. At that moment, my idea that all coaches and athletic directors were good people and looking out for each other, evaporated. So, began the paranoia and untrusting outlook I adopted from that day forward. I now knew what C.Y.A. stood for.

"How did I get here?" I asked myself. I was just at one of the biggest, most prestigious Division I programs in the country and 11 months later I'm out of a job. Cruel profession? Yes, it can be. It comes with the territory and, if you don't know that from the get go, you had better proceed with caution.

Grand Forks, North Dakota, became my next stop with newly-appointed Coach, Rich Glas. I assisted Rich on the road in returning this program back into the giant it once was under Dave Gunther. A finer coach and person would be hard to find. In a matter of months under Rich's leadership, we began to move forward, changing the culture and our recruiting approach. We assembled a class of future champions, including Ben Jacobson, now head basketball coach at the University of Northern Iowa. All league performer, Dave Vonesh, sat out during my one and only season with the Fighting Sioux. Knowing David Robertson, Chris Gardner, Steve McAndrew, and Rico Burkett were on the way lightened the mood. The team we inherited was led by Mike Boschee and Solomon Ayinla, but the supporting cast just wasn't there. We were headed to an 8-20 season so I left the team after a road loss at the University of South Dakota to go recruiting. I returned when the lakes thawed with seven new players.

This is where my career took a turn. Greener grass in Milwaukee pulled me away from Grand Forks after one year. I missed out on acquiring amazing success at the University of North Dakota by moving that spring to Marquette University in Milwaukee, Wisconsin. It was a laborious decision but in the end one of my initial three goals loomed large in my choice. Kevin O'Neill, or "KO" as he was called, was a rising superstar in coaching and was mega-connected to the basketball world. We knew each other well from spending a year together at Arizona. O'Neill arrived in Tucson, days after Wildcat Assistant Ken Burmeister took over the University of Texas-San Antonio head coaching gig. It was easy to see KO was going places quickly and I went along for the ride.

My position at North Dakota was filled by a young coach also from Iowa, Greg McDermott. The current Creighton University coach, and father of college player of the year, Doug, was a familiar face. As an assistant at Pleasant Valley High School, we played against Greg as a high schooler for Cascade. I've often wondered about those guys I worked to recruit but never coached. Obviously, they were in good hands. The new Sioux team was 57-11 over the next two seasons, making it to the Division II Elite Eight both seasons. From there Rich Glas did what he did best; he ran a first-class program and won games.

Staffing in 1990 was in the hands of the NCAA. They ruled that each program would be allowed two full-time assistant coaches and a "restricted earnings coach." Still one of the dumbest names for a hard-working college coach I can imagine, that title seemed like a good idea to the NCAA at the time. It wasn't. I received an "allowed" maximum of $12,000 a year from our summer camps to pay my paltry salary. Like it or not, I forged ahead and forgot about the money. Taking over a run-down program like Marquette was a monumental task and I was totally laser-focused on lending a hand. We worked like dogs — morning, noon, and night and eventually it paid off for KO. A grinder like none other, every day with KO was a ride. His unmatched energy was rivaled only by his Diet Coke obsession and proclivity to use the "F" word. After four seasons at Marquette and a Sweet Sixteen loss to Kentucky, he accepted the University of Tennessee Volunteers job.

The next chapter in my career began during a lunch break at our Marquette basketball camp in June 1991. KO handed me a pink phone message about a job opportunity that had just presented itself. Miami of Ohio's Joby Wright called KO to check on quality assistants for his newly-advertised job in Oxford. O'Neill said that he didn't know Wright well, but he had bumped into him quite often on the recruiting trail. O'Neill also had run into Wright's boss at Indiana, Bob Knight, at the Nike All-American camp the previous summer.

As KO rattled off zillions of details about prospects from his mezzanine perch at Princeton University, Knight looked at him and simply said, "Oh, you're one of those guys that likes this shit!" Later, Wright tracked down KO and quizzed him on important information related to the prospects.

"Hey, O'Neill, who should I be watching?" Snickering as he filled Wright in, KO had wondered how an assistant coach from one of America's great programs could walk clueless into the gym.

Listening to that one story about KO's encounter with Joby Wright, I began to get an idea of things to come with the Miami head coach. Oh, how I would experience so much more about this enigma!

I blew off the potential job opportunity at Miami for a day and then realized that because of NCAA staffing rules this was my chance to move from "restricted earnings" coach to full-time status. This would allow me to recruit off-campus, which had been my goal for several years. Recruiting is a prerequisite for climbing the ladder as an assistant in college hoops. Without it, you are looked at as less valuable to the program as a whole.

The next day I made a call to Joby and left a message, which I repeated the task four times — without a response, I assumed there was no interest on his end. Two days later I received a message that was delivered at camp with his home phone number, which was a request to call him that night.

Intrigued, I researched the situation and the positives kept stacking up. To learn the Knight system and to add *the General's* branch to my networking tree was heavy stuff. If Wright planned to turn the Redskins into NCAA participants, he would quickly shoot to a high-level job. The possibility of getting the Miami head coaching position was intoxicating.

We had a good but disjointed conversation. As I was feeling him out, he was doing the same with me. My Arizona experience with Coach Olson drew his curiosity. He blurted out three times, "So what was it like being with Burg-meister?" His reference was to Ken Burmeister, a long-time Coach Olson assistant whose relentless, bulldog style helped Iowa turn the corner and now was doing the same at Arizona. As loyal as the day is long, "Burmie" would give the shirt off his back to people he didn't know; that's the kind of guy he was. As I learned later, Joby was a classic name buster, twisting first and last names to his own liking.

For three weeks, I thought about nothing but the job. On the other hand, Wright, who was not known for his urgency, was taking his time. I began my Federal Express onslaught that KO had taught me well. Each day he received a well-thought-out package. My background, academic experience, drills, game preparation, scouting, recruiting, and organization were some of the topics I rushed to Oxford. In time, I was invited to the campus for an interview. By a long shot, it was not a conventional interview, but what was conventional about anything authored by Wright? I drove the 374 miles to Oxford, interviewed and returned to Brew City all in one day. A week later he called and offered me the job. I accepted. For the second time in 26 months my family and I were moving.

––––––––

Miami of Ohio is an academic diamond tucked in the Southwest Ohio hills. It was in the Mid-American Conference, had a bit of hoops history and carried the "Ivy League of the Midwest" moniker. When I learned of the massive football tradition, I was blown away. The Cradle of Coaches is a nickname given to Miami University in Oxford, Ohio, for producing star football coaches including greats like Paul Brown, Bo Schembechler, Woody Hayes, Weeb Eubank, Sid Gilliam, Ara Parseghian, John Pont, Jim Tressel, John Harbaugh, and Sean Payton.

*This must be a special place*, I thought. But amidst all the relocations and settling into new towns, I hadn't noticed the toll that the frequent change of jobs and locations was taking on my wife Mary Jo. She told me once that heading out to a new job is exciting but staying back and taking care of the details was difficult. It wasn't until later that I stopped to think about what that really meant.

Starting with the kids, she had her hands full. Add to it the sale of a house, saying goodbye to neighbors, contacting new doctors, dentists, and picking the right grocery store were all part of the burden she carried. For me, the excitement of diving into a new job was indescribable. Reflecting back, I really wish I had had the awareness to appreciate what my wife had done for our family during our many moves.

I experienced my share of the new town, new stationary, new players, new arena, new people, new everything. Because of Joby's history with Coach Bob Knight and the Indiana Hoosiers, I was looking forward to learning about Coach Wright. Joby was Knight's first captain in 1971 and drafted by the NBA. He became a member of Bob Knight's staff, absorbing the genius of Knight for nine seasons. During those years, he was part of NCAA championship teams in 1981 and 1987, nine NCAA tournament appearances and four Big Ten titles. As a young basketball coach from Iowa, I cut my teeth on the motion offense and fierce man-to-man defense of *The General*. The opportunity afforded me a closer glimpse into the greatest in the game. What more could I ask?

Picturesque would describe the Harvard of the Midwest, Miami of Ohio. Nestled in the hills 10 miles east of the Indiana border, it exuded tradition and academic excellence. The consistency of architecture and use of red brick was impressive to a first-time visitor. Highway 27 took me east of Richmond, Indiana, winding into this academic hamlet. Very little commercialism had hit Oxford in 1991. A bar on the outskirts of town that appeared to have experienced better days had caught my eye several years earlier. Later, I would discover that a legend named William "Bang" Meyer actually opened it from time to time. Bang became a friend and a source of encouragement to me as we got to know each other.

The Phillips 27 sign projected prominently on our left as we entered town. Although we loved Milwaukee and its ethnicity, culture and big city perks, this tiny town was a great change of pace for the Browns. The cobblestone main street with its landmark water tower extended all of three blocks. North of downtown stood Millett Hall all alone on the edge of campus. This impressive round building had witnessed the great days of Ron Harper and Coach Darryl Hedric.

Hedric, an intense and feisty coach in his day, was now an assistant athletic director who loved talking basketball and told a heck of a joke. Wayne Embry, who was an All-American player at Miami, hired Hedric as a part-time scout for the

Cleveland Cavaliers. Embry was their general manager and the job kept Coach Hedric involved in the game. He mentored me through some tough days in Oxford. Future alums Ben Roethlisberger and Wally Szczerbiak would become a part of the athletic history at Miami in the years that followed.

With each change of job and location, I caught a fresh perspective and a jolt of energy. There is something cleansing about a new environment and challenge. My office allowed me a great view of a giant lawn that separated the arena and the edge of campus. Windows encased the entire south wall at a height of 15 feet. This was truly a new look at life as a college basketball coach.

My first day in the office was filled with appointments with administration, filling out forms, and the required paperwork. A meeting with Joby took up my afternoon. Since he didn't check in until around 1:00 p.m., I assumed he had been on the golf course with boosters or giving a speech to a breakfast group in Cincinnati. How wrong I was. Joby is his own man. Jody drives Joby — no one else. He doesn't have a daily planner or office hours. Early on I learned not to ask when he was expected in the office. He didn't fill the day with 15, 30, or 60-minute segments. His philosophy was that when he shows up – he's there!

It was during the first or second day that I made an observation. It was dreadfully quiet. After the beehive of activity in Milwaukee, the absence of ringing phones all day was frightening. Welcome to *The Twilight Zone.*

Wright's first staff meeting went well. He covered expectations, things that needed immediate attention and areas of the program that needed improvement. Fellow assistant Jim Stoll sat in as we plotted our strategy for getting this program on the map again. As with every coaching job I had, I fell in love with the office. It was a place where I could spend 12-16 hours a day in comfort, complete with music and a massive white board. It didn't take long for me to love being a basketball coach in Oxford.

The first year went by fast, thanks to our success. Our roster included high character, high basketball IQ players. With Wright's defensive style and motion offense, the team became almost unbeatable. Practices were intense and purposeful. Joby's insightful approach to practice allowed him to point out key items that needed attention - he did not fill the air with yelling and criticism. He had a great way of getting his message across, sometimes at a whisper level. The quality of our practices led to great execution at game time. We were a shadow of the vintage Indiana teams with this philosophy: take care of the ball, screen the opponent to death, take good shots and defend with the best. These are the things I wanted to learn at Miami, and I am grateful for this experience as I developed significantly as a coach in those two years.

An NCAA and NIT appearance highlighted our success. A first-round 1992 NCAA game against North Carolina at Cincinnati Riverfront Coliseum put us in the national spotlight. We threw in a ton of three pointers and played Dean Smith's team to the end but eventually lost 68-63. The next season, 1993, we participated in the National Invitational Tournament, starting with an overtime win against Old Dominion. Next, we traveled to St. John's Arena in Columbus, Ohio, to take on the Ohio State Buckeyes.

Our guys played with so much grit and purpose that night, stealing one from Randy Ayers and Lawrence Funderburke. This huge win for our program propelled us to a date with John Thompson's Georgetown Hoyas. Because of scheduling complications, the home team's arena was not available. Obviously, they were planning on playing in another March event, the NCAA tournament. Unfortunately for us, the game was scheduled for George Mason University in Fairfax, Virginia. We shot the ball badly from behind the arc but had a chance down the stretch. Never one to blame the referees' calls, I felt that the NIT committee would be more excited to have the Hoyas rather than the pesky Miami of Ohio Redskins playing in the Final Four in Madison Square Garden in New York.

The end of a season creates a void that takes a week to get over. The routine of practice, game preparation, travel and games gets in your blood. A very strange, lonely feeling comes once it all abruptly ends. Such was the case after the 1992-93 season.

Postseason is the time for fast-paced recruiting and keeping an eye on the job market. At this point, I was content at Miami unless a head coach position opened up that fit my coaching skills and style. I had no thoughts of moving again until I caught wind that Joby was hunting for his next opportunity. I called Jim Stoll to find out what was going on, because I had talked to Joby very little since the conclusion of the season. He and Jim talked a lot – so, I knew he'd be 'in the know'. Jim talked around the issue and I felt something was not right. After two days, I felt both curious and left out of the equation.

It was during an unannounced visit to Joby's home that everything became clear. Fellow assistant Jim Stoll and assistant athletic director Kevin Purcell were at the kitchen counter, busy compiling lists and making calls. At this point, I went from curious to agitated. Joby was nowhere in sight but his new job was definitely job #1 for the three of them. I learned that Joby was the leading candidate for the University of Wyoming head coaching job. "Was anyone going to fill me in?" I pleaded.

Both men shrugged their shoulders, embarrassed, and the look on their faces said it all. Joby was planning his new staff and I wasn't on the list. When I asked about staffing they did not respond. The guys threw me a bone and asked if I'd start making recruiting calls to help compile a list of available players for the Cowboys to sign in the event this all worked out for them. I went to work at my home, furiously burning up the phone lines to make a point and come up with some studs I could possibly sign. The phone bill I incurred ended up being my own. Imagine that!

Call after call after call I made to Joby. Still, he obviously avoided me at all costs for reasons I will never understand. Finally, our family was tired of being held hostage to the situation. I walked the five blocks to his home and knocked on the front door. His saint-of-a-wife greeted me and ushered me to the garage. If there was ever a hand-caught-in-the-cookie-jar moment, this was it. Joby was busy wrapping up framed photographs from the 1997 National Championship game. "Hey Randy, how's it going," he asked. I was thinking, "How's it going? Are you insane; what the hell is going on?" Instead, I attempted the high road and asked him how things were going for him. When I told Joby I wanted to know about this secret job, a puzzled look from Joby turned up my anger meter. Sarcastically I asked if my work, game preparation, recruiting, public relations, practice coaching, game time performance, or the two Mid-American Conference titles, an NCAA and NIT appearance had anything to do with being kept in the dark about his career shift.

"I do want to talk with you about going to Wyoming, so let's do this. Meet me in my office tomorrow morning at 8:00 a.m., okay?" I thought about offering to pick him up on the way to the office but decided against it. I knew I would never see the guy again. The odds of Joby making this meeting were less than me winning the Masters that year. Totally baffled, I showed up at 7:40 a.m. the next morning in the office. At 8:10 a.m., I called his house. When his mother-in-law picked up the phone, I learned he wouldn't be meeting me in the office as planned. "Joby left on a flight this morning to take the job at Wyoming," she told me. To this day I have not heard from him nor seen him. It is one of the most amazing things I could ever imagine happening. Feelings of anger, confusion, and betrayal ruled the day. Yet, when you look at my entire body of work, it fits rather nicely.

———

For the second time in six years, I was unemployed. Fortunately, co-assistant at Miami, Brian Donoher, was crucial in helping me jump onto the new staff at Stetson University in

Deland, Florida. Brian's father, Don, was a legendary coach at the University of Dayton and was inducted in 2015 into the National Collegiate Basketball Hall of Fame. Brian, a great young guy and basketball junkie, and I drove south, the radio cranking out the sounds of a band that was new to me, *Hootie and the Blowfish*. My new boss Dan Hipsher was a shrewd ball coach with a big-time sense of humor and a mean golf game. I'll always be indebted to him for hiring me and asking me to join his staff in Florida. Hip had a feel for running a successful program and that's exactly what he did. After two successful seasons by Stetson standards, he returned to his Ohio roots to accept a job at the University of Akron. I found myself on the road recruiting the day I found out that he had accepted the Akron job. In quick fashion, I was handed the head coaching job by Athletic Director Bob Jacoby. Cloud nine ensued. A press conference and the words "head coach" after my name seemed like a dream. This was the second of my goals that I'd accomplished and I was ready for the challenge, thanks to Dan Hipsher. Fittingly, all I remember about the press conference is my two-year-old Natalie reaching for a ball perched just below the podium. That memory has become increasingly special through time, especially since 1998. The next task was to fill my staff as quickly as possible with guys who shared my vision, passion, and ability to work long into the night.

———

Loyal and eager, we embarked on a journey to get the Stetson Hatters to their first ever NCAA Tournament. We worked relentlessly on campus and the recruiting trail. There never seemed to be enough time to do what I thought had to be done. The fun factor was high as well. A few late nights at McCabe's Pub were followed by early morning team lifting sessions.

Separated by a few hours, the two facilities sat next door from each other.

I told my assistant Jeff Rutter many times, "We could have just slept in the car."

Jeff Rutter Scott Shreffler, Rico Burkett, and Jonas Beugen were stars and worked like there was no tomorrow. No one on that campus knew what kind of staff I had assembled. I knew this group of working hard, playing hard coaches would get the job done with the Hatters. Rutter became the head coach at the University of Wisconsin-Parkside after just one year. An incredible A to Z guy, Rutt could tell you the top five eighth-graders in Alaska that were left-handed at a moment's notice. He later served as Greg McDermott's assistant at Northern Iowa and Iowa State and stayed in Ames to work for Fred Hoiberg. Next, he was the top assistant at Drake University and served as head coach the final 20 games of the 2016-2007 season. Currently, Jeff is an assistant coach at, you guessed it, Miami of Ohio. Full Circle! After one year, Scott Shreffler returned as an assistant to his alma mater, Evansville. "Mr. Motion" has a keen sense for teaching the game. Rico Burkett was the crown jewel that I plucked out of Iowa Central Community College in my hometown of Fort Dodge, to run the show at North Dakota. I regret not having the opportunity to coach Rico. A phenomenal defender, leader, and competitor, his persona was the glue needed in Grand Forks. Rico went on to become the head coach at Wayne State College in Nebraska. As for Beugen, I think I wore him out as he headed back to his home state of Minnesota. The silver lining was that Jonas met his future wife that year in Deland!

Looking back, I would have taken that staff of three with me anywhere in the country. We all wish we would have caught a break at Stetson, but life had other plans for each of us. There are some fundamental leadership decisions I would change, but overall, I felt we were on the right path regardless of obstacles. Unfortunately, a decision to limit the recruitment of Junior College players due to extremely high private school admission requirements derailed our early efforts. We're at an NCAA Division I school and we can't recruit Junior College players. "They don't have good enough grades to get into Stetson," they told me. "Really?" I said. That's why they're

JUCOS! We needed ready-made players with a valuable two years of play behind them to walk on campus. To get this program into *The Big Dance*, we needed difference makers.

It was the end of year two and we were charging forward. We were not playing with a full deck athletically. In terms of skills, basketball IQ and high character, we excelled. I loved the players we had brought to Deland, but we faced an obstacle without the right blend of talent. Halfway through my second season as head coach, I sensed the unexplainable. Things just didn't feel right to me. I remember feeling like we were being set aside because we wanted to win too badly but, in reality, we were driven, serious and tireless in our approach and I was doing exactly what I was hired to do.

Somewhere I've heard it said, "I can't see a single storm cloud in the sky, but I sure can smell the rain." After recruiting in Texas for five days, I returned to campus for staff meetings and more recruiting. Athletic Director Jeff Altier asked me to come to his office to discuss next year's schedule. It was one of those frozen moments in my life that I can't erase. There was no talk of scheduling at all. I was tricked into a meeting that would be my last as the head coach at Stetson University. I walked in to find the women's athletic director in the office as well. Instant red lights!

The conversation was filled with comments like, "Going in a different direction," "We appreciate your efforts," and "If there's anything we can do......." My immediate thought was, "Here's what you can do. You can talk about scheduling and then let me go back upstairs and get to the job of building the program." I begged for specifics as to why I was being let go, but received none. Without being given a reason for my dismissal, I hauled myself home again to drop the news on Mary Jo and the girls. Our life was taking a different direction... yet again. For the first time since I was a 20-year-old college student, I was out of coaching. I felt like John Corabi when he filled in for Vince Neil as lead singer for Motley Crue. Aerosmith's Steven Tyler laughed and said, "So, you're the one who's getting ready to be shot out of the canon."

# Chapter Eight
# Meredith

In 1992, at the age of 35, on an ordinary fall day, I experienced the unimaginable—the death of our beautiful daughter, Meredith, which drastically changed my life. No longer was I innocent enough to believe that we controlled our destiny. No longer did I trust as I once had. No longer did I ~~happens~~ believe God. I was angry with God and let Him know it constantly. Every facet of life — from breathing to eating to relaxing to working — changed forever. Meredith passed away on November 29, exactly one day after her fourth birthday. Our hearts were ripped in two, and even now, I find that some days the hollowness of my daughter's death makes life seem dreary.

If there is a manual on dealing with the death of your child in a healthy way, I didn't get a copy. There is no such guide on how to pick yourself up off this type of floor and move forward. How do you deal with tragedy? I was clueless, and to an extent, I still feel that way even today 25 years later.

The death of our children is a very sensitive and emotional subject for me, and rightly so. By being vulnerable and sharing the story of two of my daughters' deaths, I relive the pain and turmoil of those times. However, I share their deaths with you, my readers, in hopes of bringing you a spark of hope during your own adversity, whatever that may be.

---

Our daughter Meredith was born on November 28, 1988, in Grand Forks, North Dakota on a horrible November day in terms of weather. It was subzero wind chill the day we brought her home. She was the first grandkid in our family on both sides so, she was pretty precious. Since her birth, Meredith got a chance to live in North Dakota, then Wisconsin, and then

Ohio. So, in her four years and one day, she lived in three different states.

The day after Meredith's fourth birthday was much like any other day. My last time with her was before I left the house to go to team practice. I was coaching at Miami of Ohio and I asked her if she wanted me to stop at the store and get her anything. Meredith gave me a brief list and I remember writing it down (I still have the note) on our basketball stationery and tucking it in my pocket, and then, as usual, off to practice I went.

My wife, Mary Jo, and I had zero awareness that anything was awry when I left the house. Meredith was completely normal except she had a bit of a cold that day, but nothing out of the ordinary. Like any other day, I went to practice, assuming my family would be intact and healthy when I came home later that day. That's how I went into the day.

Somewhere in the midst of practice, I was on the north end of the court conducting a drill and I saw a man walking into the arena from my right, and walking toward the court. I didn't think twice about it but then the guy got closer and closer. He then walked onto the floor and I thought it was weird for him to just walk onto the court like that. As I turned, I became aware that it was a campus security staff person, and my heart dropped. He walked briskly, wearing a University Public Safety jacket, with a serious look on his face. While still approaching, the stranger looked me right in the eye. I asked, "Is there something I can help you with?"

The man then inquired, "Are you Randy Brown?"

I answered, "Yes, I am."

He said, "You need to come with me." That's a horrible thing to hear.

I responded, "Well, I really can't because we're in the middle of practice."

The security person then demanded, "No, you don't understand, you have to come with me."

I told one of the coaches that this guy had come for me and that I had to take off. I followed him out to his squad car and asked him, "What's the deal?"

Though unwilling to delve into specifics, only that he was just alerted to come pick me up and take me with him (he didn't even tell me where we were going). I begged for him to tell me what was happening and where we were going.

All he said was, "We're just going up here a couple of blocks and I'll drop you off."

I knew the way to the hospital and when he took that final turn, a thought blasted through me, "Oh No!" I ran through the front doors and the nurses guided me to where I needed to go. My wife, obviously in shock, was there; she had a hollow, blank look on her face. I don't remember much from that point. All I remember was that our daughter was laying on the hospital bed and she had already passed.

I spoke to her as if she was able to hear; it's all I could do.

Meredith's death was just that sudden.

I had left home, gone to practice for less than two hours, then boom, my entire life had changed in an instant. My wife and I were in so much shock. The nursing staff kept saying softly, "I'm sorry. She passed away a few minutes ago; she quit breathing."

Mary Jo was trying to explain everything to me and I just wasn't getting it. I was trying to get Meredith to talk because there were some things I wanted to tell her that I hadn't had a chance to, because who would've thought? Afterward, we went through an autopsy and initially, they called the cause of death or COD was Guillain-Barre; I think that's what the death certificate even says.

Our daughter Claire was born on November 20, 1991 and she was about a year old when her sister passed, so of course we were worried about her, too, overprotective you might say. We would have kept her in a bubble if that had been possible.

We went on a fact-finding mission and tried to find the underlying cause of what had just happened. Eventually, we connected with Dr. Katherine Mathews, MD, who was a child neurologist at the University of Iowa Children's Hospital. Dr. Mathews helped us learn the disease was called Familial Paroxysomal Rhabdomyolysis. But essentially, the thing that was so difficult for us, was that they couldn't tell us why our daughter died or what the actual cause of her death was, other than what was on her death certificate. We did learn that she had elevated potassium levels that can cause heart failure. These levels are a side effect and a complication of acute rhabdo. Further down the road, when they came upon some type of diagnosis of what it was, they couldn't tell us how to prevent it, or even what to look for in order to help prevent future problems. It was kind of like – wait for it to happen again and do your best. That's how we felt. "God, what's the wisdom in all of this," I pleaded.

Witnessing your daughter lying dead in a hospital bed doesn't seem real. You're in shock. You're trying to make sense of it all. You're just hoping to hell that you wake up any second. But I never woke up. I think I yelled at the doctor, "Isn't there something you can do? My daughter was fine when I left the house and you can't even tell me why she died!" It's one of those situations where you kind of go crazy because you want answers. I wanted an answer and I didn't have one. They didn't give us one. *Don't make sense :(*

We were also trying to determine whether it was a neuromuscular disorder or a disease. The doctors suggested we both carried a recessive gene for the girls to inherit but we had no knowledge of previous family history. In the end, three of our four daughters ended up having it, which is crazy odds for something that is as rare as this particular disease is supposed to be.

The shock of Meredith passing so suddenly and people coming to the house was something we became accustomed to. The experience of having to entertain and talk to people when you'd rather be screaming or curling up in a ball is just so wearing on a person going through something like we did. Every close friend, and we had a lot of them, thank goodness, is calling the house, and you don't want to blow them off, you want to talk to them, but as soon as you start talking, they might have their own questions or proposed answers about what happened. They asked all the same questions with the greatest intentions; it was like I could turn on a tape recorder. We were in a fog for days.

Honestly, I don't remember much. I do remember my family being there. I do remember preparing for the service. At the local Methodist church, we had a memorial service, then headed back to Fort Dodge, Iowa, our hometown. I must say, I'm just not real big on the overall burial ceremony. I mean, there's a child who was cremated, yet – there's a stone in the ground that indicates that this is where she's laid to rest. I don't know. I guess you just kind of go through the formality of burials out of respect or tradition.

Even though I don't quite recall the time table, we eventually returned to Oxford, Ohio. I remember thinking, "How am I ever going to face my team and coaches? How am I ever going to be able to face people in the community? How long is it going to take before I return to practice?" I just didn't think I would be able to function, and to tell the truth, by this time, I really wasn't functioning. I waited a week but that wasn't long enough. It was about 10 days or so, in the middle of practice that I snuck into the arena unannounced, and went way up top and watched the practice. Finally, I cried.

I was so afraid to go down on that floor, though it was one of the things I loved the most. I knew I had a job and a responsibility, yet I felt strongly that I would forget my daughter if I went back to work. Of course, the typical response was, "Meredith would want you to go back to practice."

So, I eventually returned to some sort of normalcy of life – such as being at practice with everyone who continued to ask about me and wanted to know how we were coping with Meredith's death.

An extraordinarily special group of young people were on that team, and they were amazing. They welcomed me back and we kind of got started again.

I'll share a very poignant letter I received from one of the players at the end of this chapter.

During the same time, as I returned to work, Mary Jo and I went to Cincinnati to Compassionate Friends meetings. Compassionate Friends is a national wellness and recovery group for people who have lost children. The meetings were okay and we attended regularly for a few months. There were a lot of other people who were hurting as well; though there was no real healing, just sharing and listening. After a few meetings, we just kind of grieved on our own. I dreaded grief, or what I knew of it. I knew there was deep pain to experience for a long time. A better plan was to work, keep Meredith on my heart, and dive back into work.

On the heels of finding out more about the disease, not knowing what it was or how to prevent it, we walked on eggshells for a long, long time with our daughter Claire. Mary Jo especially, because she was at home, facing our problems head-on. I always had an escape, and most of the time that consisted of going to work, practice, recruiting, and games. The mistake I made was just adding hours upon hours upon hours to my day. Work became my grief relief. I worked an insane number of hours – anytime I had a chance to go out of town to recruit or scout a game, I did. What appeared as work was actually running from reality. The problem with running is that you're always being chased by one who never tires. Ever! A good example for an addict would be knowing a common recovery statement such as, "Remember, your addict is always in the corner doing pushups.

So, I had to keep running. My mind told me – that if I stopped, I'd collapse, and the last thing I wanted to do was to fall apart. I thought I would absolutely fall to pieces and never be able to get up if I had to face the hurt and feel the pain. There's all the guilt that a parent experiences: "What could I have done differently, what didn't I do." Thus, I found that if it was 11:00 p.m. and I was on the way home, I'd stop at a bar, whether by myself or with a buddy; I just wanted to sit and have some beers. Alcohol always took me to a place where things were just a little bit better...at least temporarily. Beer and music in a dark bar were a desirable elixir. I'm not talking about a drunken state, but if I could drink enough to get myself into a place where I could temporarily smile, even slightly, then I felt like life was okay. Did you notice the word "temporarily?" That's exactly what it was... temporary.

For the longest time, I didn't feel like I was supposed to smile or laugh because I thought it meant that I was forgetting about Meredith. I would catch myself smiling at something and I would feel so horrible. It was like in some respects, you want your life to end because you don't think you will ever again feel joy. You don't feel like you can ever trust anybody, including God. You just want to numb yourself. I can tell you it's a horrible existence – the thought that you don't want to live anymore – you're carrying all that on your shoulders.

As a couple, Mary Jo and I talked, but you know, there was not a lot of depth to our conversations because we did not know how to grieve together. There's no manual that sums up grieving individually and as a couple, in a tidy paint-by-number package, so she and I sort of grieved in our own separate ways. Actually, my grief was deep but dealing with it was on the surface. Investing into the entire process of peeling away the layers didn't motivate me at all. Later, I paid the price.

My wife and I learned about the five stages of grieving, and while I do think it works to educate yourself about it, it takes a combination of pain, surrender, and trust. You should lean on your faith because nothing else makes sense – zero. And when you are angry with your Maker it's impossible to move forward. That, too, takes time!

I would look at my Mom and Dad and ask in desperation, "How could she die? How come Meredith's not here anymore?" For my parents to look at their son in such pain and tell me they didn't know had to be excruciating. That was so scary for me because moms and dads are supposed to have all the answers. My parents provided as much emotional support as they could muster. Anything Mary Jo and I needed, our parents were there for us, and I will always be thankful for that.

Well-meaning friends said things like, "You have to move on," and "You can't stay in the past," but none of that stuff fit for me. None of it caused me to feel comforted. What if somebody in the community catches me laughing about something? I was very sensitive about that. So, just being on my own, not really observing my own actions, I began to self-soothe. That's the course I took.

Allow me to backtrack for a moment and get into the disease of Familial Paroxysmal Rhabdoymyolysis just a little bit. Meredith, who had just turned four-years-old the previous day, was at home with my wife and she had a cough. I'm not sure if she complained about a sore stomach, but Mary Jo put her on the toilet. Within about five minutes, Mary Jo heard Meredith screaming for her. She ran upstairs and saw that Meredith had slipped through the toilet and was half way down, just kind of folded up. Her muscles were just gone.

As I understand it now, the immune system is attacked, breaking down the muscle tissue that attacks major organs – then it's just a matter of time. I mean, she was fine the day before. As I said, it was her birthday and she was the happiest kid in the world.

We tried to figure out as much as possible about the disease that took our first daughter from us and my wife and I tried to learn what we needed to do to keep Claire healthy.

A year later we moved to Florida, and Natalie, our third daughter, was born on April 8, 1994. Our daughter Jane was also born in Florida, two years later on November 27, 1996. We now had three daughters for the first time; Claire, Natalie, and Jane.

Once we relocated to Florida, we learned more about the disease and what it entailed because Claire got sick. Shortly after Mary Jo and the girls returned from a wedding in Iowa, on November 23, 1994, Claire showed symptoms similar to Meredith's and was taken to Arnold Palmer Children's

Hospital in Orlando. She didn't get sick just that once though, she got sick three times. We thought we had lost her once, then the second time was even more horrifying than the first. She was admitted again on March 3, 1995 and didn't return home until April 5th. Mary Jo and I took our daughter to the hospital for preventative treatment the third time, and then to a local doctor a few other times. I cannot recall exactly how many times we sought help for Claire, but it was often. On the occasions when Claire got sick, Mary Jo and I would sit and glance over at each other as if to say, "Should we or shouldn't we take her?" We always chose to take her in if she seemed sick in any way. Having your child's life hanging in the balance every day is a curse that no couple should have to endure. Claire and Jane have become amazing daughters, both with a little extra smile and a thankfulness that they are healthy. We are blessed to have them.

When I needed to travel somewhere I always tried to say something special to my daughters, spend a little time with them, hoping they weren't sleeping when I needed to leave. I didn't want to repeat the experience with Meredith when I wasn't able to talk to her again, to tell her the things I needed to tell her. Every time Claire got sick, we'd ask ourselves if this was simply a normal kid with a runny nose and lacking an appetite, or was it a kid who was minutes from dying. Because of how quickly Meredith died – our emotions were not always in check.

I carried information about the disease and hospital paperwork with me everywhere I went for fear I'd have to run to an emergency room for Claire. I remember at one point running in the hospital doors saying, "This is it, this is what you have to do." I would grab the staff as they tried to calm me down. It was like a medical drama you'd watch on television. The staff didn't seem to understand the gravity of the situation as I shouted to them, "Her sister died from this; here's what you have to give her! Here's a list of the five things you have to give her right now!"

We are really lucky to have Claire still with us. At one point, each of her legs blew up probably four times their size. They looked like two huge tree trunks. It was horrifying. I thought her legs were going to pop. They had to make incisions on her lower leg about six inches long on each side to release the pressure, a procedure known as fasciotomy. The hope was to relieve pressure and reduce the chance of permanent nerve damage.

Emergency room visits were tough because even if we called in ahead of time and told them what the disease was and what to prepare for, they usually didn't know exactly how to handle our daughter's illness — they couldn't prepare because they had no idea. When we finally did get the definitive paperwork on how to react, what the response protocol was and what they needed in terms of drugs and such, it was a little bit easier but I remember a couple of times going in there waving my papers through the air — they thought I was a mad man.

The first thing we always asked was, "What's her potassium number?" In Orlando, we felt good because Arnold Palmer Children's Hospital is a world-class children's hospital. When we came back the second time they were familiar with our case so their response time was faster and better because they knew what they were dealing with and were able to take care of Claire better. Each time we had to return to the hospital, my mind flashed, "Oh my gosh, come on." You turn around and there are your parents. You turn around and there are your in-laws. You turn around and there are your friends. And you're explaining what happened... again. Didn't we go through this once? Such déjà vu.

ER's have a process that they need to go through and I'm sure they are trained to not yell back and to remain very calm, "Here's what we need to do. We need to get her looked at and an IV inserted, etc." And I'd yell, "No! You can't waste time, she could be dead in a matter of four minutes!" I'm going on and on because Claire could have literally died within minutes. We had to trust the doctors. When a doctor would come back to us

and say he had never heard of Familial Paroxysmal Rhabdoymyolysis, I usually responded, "You've got to be kidding me?"
At that point, we felt like we knew the disease so well. It's the
same way people become experts at cancer because they deal
with it with family members and friends. That's kind of like
how we felt.

Our daughter Claire is a warrior. She truly is. She has a
different heart than any kid I've ever known. She's so gentle
and kind; she'll pray for people she doesn't even know. I don't
think Claire could have ever been an athlete because of her low
muscle tone. She walks fine but she's really just kind of weak
in general. She's cautious but it's obvious why; two of her
siblings have died and she's almost died, so you can't wonder
why Claire's so cautious. It's her right. Fortunately, Jane was
never presented with the disease. We lived on the edge with
her but are so blessed we didn't have to repeat the experience
with her. She is so kind, loving, and accepting. Deep down I
know she and Claire have had to deal with their own
perception of their childhood and repeated difficulty. Based on
all of this, they are amazing daughters.

I confess to you: this chapter was extremely painful to
write; to remember those stormy, dark days of death, grieving,
depression, and loss. But, I'd like to end this chapter on a
positive note with the letter I spoke about earlier. The one I
received from one of my players, Craig Michaelis, the day after
Meredith died (November 29, 1992).

*Dear Coach Brown and Family,*

*I want you to know that you are in my daily prayers. May
you be granted the grace and peace to be strong, and I want you
to know that it is our turn to be strong for you. If you need
anything, please call. You know, in God's grand scheme, things
often happen that aren't justified, measurable, or even
understandable. His ways are often confusing. Here is a verse I
like to keep in my locker that keeps me strong in my times of*

*need. I know words cannot make your heart lighter but I hope this verse is able to give you some strength.*

> *"Trust in the Lord with all thine heart; and lean not into thine own understanding. In all thy ways acknowledge him, and he shall direct thy paths."*
>
> Proverbs 3:5-6

Love, Craig

# Chapter Nine
## Natalie

The sting of being fired at Stetson was deep for me and my family.

The opportunity in Deland represented a 12-year journey, from high school JV coach to running my own Division I program as the head coach. It was much more than a coaching job, it was the culmination of a lifelong dream.

In June of 1997, we moved back to Iowa and settled down in Cedar Falls. Through raising our four girls and dealing with Claire's health emergencies, it was our goal to stay in the college game. I interviewed for two jobs, but could not find one that fit. I'd been a head coach and I wanted to continue to be a head coach. My interviews at Southwest Minnesota State and University of Minnesota-Mankato got my blood pumping and my hopes surged. Unfortunately, I was the runner-up for both jobs... so, I headed back to Cedar Falls with my tail between my legs. There were other opportunities but my heart told me "no". It was my mental health, not my heart that was actually making the call.

Now without a job, faithful Mary Jo headed out to the outside world to work and dutifully support our family. I secretly thought, "I could never meet each day the way she does." I stayed at home and played Mr. Mom.

I didn't know at the time that I was struggling with depression. There were times when I had to convince myself to rise and face the day—I knew there were three smiling faces who would soon greet me. My new team consisted of six-year-old Claire, three-year-old Natalie, and five-month-old Jane.

Playing Mr. Mom to our three beautiful girls was my saving grace. Those three angelic faces could brighten anyone's life. The girls were my most precious gifts each day and this Mr. Mom way of life was a new experience for a driven, accomplishment-hungry coach like me. Claire was in kindergarten at Orchard Hill Elementary just three blocks from our home, so, I dropped her off first, and then I dropped Natalie off next at Farmstead Preschool which was north of Cedar Falls city limits. Horses, pigs, and chickens were part of Farmstead's unique curriculum, and the farm setting provided a great experience for her. I could see her bright eyes light up as she patiently sat on the designated wooden bench, waiting to be picked up at the end of the day.

The big event each day was picking up "Sissy" at school at 3:00 p.m.

The look on Natalie and baby Jane's face as their big sister Claire spotted us and climbed into the van was priceless.

Our after-school routine was complete with a snack and talk of each daughter's school day. We had a special game the girls loved. We took turns describing the day outside, using words to colorfully portray the weather. Natalie went first, then Claire and then me. Baby Jane, whose face was covered with squashed carrots and peas, stared in amazement at what was going on. "It's a big, blue, wonderful day," Natalie would proudly exclaim. Claire would follow with, "The wind blows on a cold, blustery day." I felt outmatched on many days. Oh, how I wish I could have ONE of those days back. I was fooled into thinking the girls would all remain healthy for the rest of their childhood. It was my hope more than my common sense.

Each school and workday ended at 5:30 p.m., when their mom got home... the girls would rush to be with her. Relieved, I would assume my duties were over and go into isolation mode—rarely sharing my feelings or thoughts, my greeting was forced, at best. While Mary Jo and the girls bonded through conversation about their day, I looked forward to my daily walk which weaved in and out of the neighborhood. I would go along the walking trails of Cedar Falls. For weeks in a row, I listened to the same bootleg Chris Duarte tape at maximum levels. My 80-minute walking concert each afternoon allowed me to escape the reality of life. It was my piece of sanity and tranquility.

My walking stride was confident and my energy level rose as the sounds of "My Way Down" screamed from my headphones. Duarte, an up and coming guitar genius from Austin, Texas, was my personal savior that fall. His talent and creativity put him in a class of the best guitar players in the world. We've since become friends and at opportune moments I've shared a lot about my life with him. I've told him dozens of times how much his music means to me, now, and during the darkest of times. Seeing him play during a live concert invigorates me because of his creativeness, drive, and commitment to putting on a memorable show. Chris Duarte is a one in a million and I appreciate his friendship.

## Another Fateful Day

On February 1, 1998, we got quite a bit of snow and the girls and I were outside, playing. I remember watching Natalie; she was super active and kind of a *sparkplug*. She probably would have been our best athlete if I was to project forward. She was really spontaneous and didn't seem to worry about anything. The four of us were all over that snow. At that time, Natalie was three years and ten months. The next morning, Mary Jo said she didn't think we should send Claire to kindergarten. Claire didn't look right. That was always our deal, "Claire doesn't look right." And that would just scare the hell out of us. We could tell, sometimes in an instant, if she didn't look right... but, at the same time, we would stay very vigilant and extremely ready. Well, on this morning, we talked about keeping her home because of that look, and we did. Mary Jo ran to HyVee to purchase some liquid for Claire before work. "Claire, you're going to stay home today." The girls and I ate breakfast and I sent them to play downstairs.

We had a Lazy Boy recliner and all three of them were sitting right in a row 1-2-3 in the Lazy Boy watching a Disney movie. I was going back and forth doing household chores and all three daughters were as content as could be. I don't remember the timetable, but after maybe an hour, I checked on Claire, which I did quite frequently. "Claire how are you doing?" "Good. Good." She was fine.

Then I looked at Natalie and my first thought was, *she's going to die.* She looked horrible. She had "the look." I grabbed her and asked her some questions. She didn't respond. I said, "Natalie, come on. Come on." I knew right then and there – her face had turned whitish, though her pallor was normally light anyway. She just looked pale.

I called 911 and I called my wife. From there, everything was an absolute horror story. Natalie was conscience when they got her to Waterloo. We couldn't go in the ambulance so we had to drive. I believe the staff at Waterloo could have saved her life. I really do. We were not pleased with the people at Waterloo because they acted as if they knew the answers despite us trying to tell them what needed to be done. They decided it would be best to life-flight her to Iowa City.

At this time, Natalie was conscience but not really responding very well, which caused us to have to drive because we weren't allowed to go on the plane. The 80-minute drive was the trip from hell and one of the most hopeless times of my life. Mary Jo's school psych supervisor, Dennis Sinclair, drove us in our van to Iowa City. The car seemed to move like molasses down the road. *Will she be able to talk to us when we get there? Will she be able to talk? Will she be alive?*

Maybe it was too late, but we felt something could have been done to save Natalie's life when she arrived at University of Iowa Hospital. My wife and I were just two parents questioning everything but we had a sense that something was not right in the way our daughter was being handled. After Meredith's death, it was hard to trust anyone!

We finally arrived and discovered right away that our daughter wasn't doing well. The staff was trying all sorts of procedures to save Natalie's life. They tried to resuscitate her and I knew she was gone.

Brother Roger and his wife, Jackie, stood close in support and pain. I remember picking up the phone in the hospital waiting room and throwing it against the wall as hard as I could into a picture frame. I kicked over a garbage can too. With the death of my daughter, Natalie, I absolutely flipped. That's about all I remember.

All I could think was, "Oh God, it's happened again."

Natalie was within two months of Meredith's age when she passed. Our reality was Déjà vu all over again. The same sympathy cards. The same people. The same calls. The same casseroles. The same hugs. The same tears. Again, it was back to Fort Dodge to bury another daughter. The same shock coming back from the services.

I was spent. I was gone. By this time, I was absolutely gone and so we were really kind of operating on a thin emotional thread. Our family made minimal efforts to comfort each other. Shock and numbness ruled the day.

# Chapter Ten
# Ear Shattering Silence

When driving into Iowa City on 2nd Street, a right turn onto Hawkins Drive will take you uphill on a curving road past Carver Hawkeye Arena and Duane Banks Field. Down and then up another hill, Hawkins Drive intersects with Evashevski Drive at a stoplight. From that intersection looking south I'm brought to my knees. I've walked every street in this town at one time or another.

But it's this one block-long stretch of street that has profound meaning. In this spot, you can always hear the roar of the crowd as the Hawkeyes score another touchdown. The sound rushes out of the stadium and pours onto the traffic surrounding Nile Kinnick Stadium. Goosebump memories by the thousands were born on the west side of this street ever since my first game in 1969. Never on this earth will I know of a spot like this one on Hawkins and Evashevski. I celebrate six Saturdays each fall on the west side of the street, screaming for the good guys to win. Sharing a lifetime of memories with my ballgame partner, Scott Nelson. I cast my eyes to the east each Saturday for a brief moment. The sights, sounds, and smells are still fresh.

I find it peculiar how one solitary street surrounded by two worlds can be diametrically opposed to each other.

The left side of the street is soundless, beyond quiet... eerie almost. It is a world of bustling people using technology and education to heal those in need. The University of Iowa hospitals are recognized across the country for excellence and research. They are in the business of hope and healing. For the past 22 years though, I've not heard a sound from it. Sadness can move at 100 miles per hour—a deep breath, then another, as I attempt to squeeze out a smile her way.

Natalie Jean Brown, 3 ½-years-old, took her last breath in the emergency room on a grief-stricken night in February 1998.

Talk about being on a rollercoaster of life! Mary Jo and I had one child, then we had two, then we had one, then we had two, then we had three, and then we had two. Being a former math teacher, those numbers just didn't add up for us.

My wife and I looked at the two beautiful daughters who were still with us: Claire and Jane. At the time, Jane was young so she doesn't remember any of what happened but Claire had just seen her second sister die and then disappear. We were extremely scared for Claire because she had already presented symptoms of the same disease. Man, there were days I just wanted to check out so badly, yet, still knowing I couldn't. It was too much...it was just way too much.

Claire, who has such a tender, beautiful heart, would ask us questions and it would just break our hearts. She'd ask, "Well does that mean if they are up in heaven together that they know each other? Can they play with each other? Can we get any of their toys to them?"

When you're a kid, all you've got is your parents, and Claire will tell you that she remembers a lot of what happened but I'm sure at the time she just passed it off to whatever we were telling her; she listened to our explanations and accepted her life as just the way it was. Still, Claire's questions and thoughts continued, "And I'm scared because I've been sick and Natalie just died because she got sick. How come I get sick a lot and I haven't died? Does that mean Jane is going to die?" We did the best we could to answer her innocent questions while at the same time, dealing with our own overwhelming grief. We had a book or two featuring animals that died and went to heaven and that helped to explain the process.

Claire is now 25. She'll get teary-eyed if she gets a sore throat or a slight fever. Not like a terrorized type of tears but just real paranoid and a little scared. I understand why she feels that way because nobody ever told us that the disease goes away with age. Claire knows enough to call and ask what to do. Or, if she can't get ahold of either of us, she knows to get to the hospital. Now that Claire's 25, she can make that decision. At age nine, she couldn't do that but we were there to make that decision for her. Other than Claire being hospitalized in Iowa City in second grade, January 2000, between the ages of three and a half and six were the ages when everything happened. We had to be on guard 24/7. Our daughter Jane has never presented symptoms of the disease throughout her entire life of 20 years as of this writing, and for that, we're very thankful.

## Just Too Much

I'm sure I don't realize how much stress and strain my wife went through with everything before we moved back to Iowa. I was in a job where I was traveling, not usually home for dinner, and often not home until late. She had an amazing responsibility knowing that if one of the girls got sick in the middle of swimming lessons, she had to be there and get her to the hospital – I mean every second of wherever they were, Mary Jo had to be ready to spring into action. I'm sure I never really appreciated that responsibility she bore.

Now, post-divorce, our communication remains limited. We discuss our daughters; that's about it. It's me that struggles with being single now. Mary Jo has a more light-hearted approach to our 32-year split. I'm still mad. Anger and frustration linger from going separate ways. Being prideful gets in the way, but a sense of losing my family lingers. Not in the true sense, but in the "today" sense. I'm alone because the kids live at our home with Mary Jo. It's a new life albeit lonely at times.

-----

At this writing, our daughter Jane, who attends the University of Iowa, is a junior. College hasn't been easy for her but she seems to be doing better now. She's got some anxiety issues, so we keep a protective and loving eye on her. I often wonder how much of the past has affected the girls in present day. Both are a bit cautious and it's easy to see why. One thing is certain, they love the Lord, their parents, and their extended family. Who can ask for more than that?

I'm the first to admit that one of my crutches is my pride and I'm holding onto it big time because I just don't want it to be okay. It's a lot like not smiling. The divorce wasn't okay with me because it wasn't my choice. Hence, the acceptance part is really hard for me.

———

Mary Jo wants to be friends but I told her, "I'd rather still be married, I don't really need your friendship." That seems really whacked out to me that she tells me she needs me as a friend now when I wasn't good enough as a husband when we were married. I don't know, something about that doesn't make sense to me. So down the road, maybe.

Every day my heart will get a little softer toward her because I'm beginning to realize just how much she had to go through on her end of our relationship and on her end of taking care of our daughters. I'm taking time to reflect upon how much I may have taken my wife... the mother of our daughters, for granted, my being gone a lot and knowing what she had to shoulder.

Mary Jo chose to live two years while I, her husband, was in prison. We knew a lot of people. I was a public figure in our community. What that was like for her, I have no idea. What it was like to visit her husband in prison, bring her kids with her, the whole deal. As an inmate, I didn't give it much credence to be honest with you until now that I'm reflecting on our divorce, what it was really like for her. After all, we were married for 32 years. There will come a time when I will communicate my thoughts to her...but that time is not today.

Each time I pay a bill, I think about what it's like to split resources, finances; that's a daunting task and it is sobering. I never paid attention to our savings, I just knew we were in decent shape. It's funny because you get me in front of somebody else and I'm a really good coach, but I don't do a very good job of coaching my own self. It's easier to coach and mentor somebody else than it is to ask if I am listening to myself. What would my life look like if I did what I just told a player or peer to do? That's almost like a slap in the face, a wake-up call.

Soon, I was about to experience the biggest wake-up call of my life.

# Chapter Eleven
# Oh, What a Tangled Web I Weaved

*"He who mounts the tiger finds it difficult to dismount."*

**~ Rudyard Kipling**

The fall of 1997 began a year of new horizons. Instead of flying out of the house early for the office, I was Mr. Mom getting breakfast for the girls. In the back of my mind, I felt a nudge but couldn't identify it. Soon enough I realized I didn't have the office and the rush of the game to pacify me 24 hours at a time. The nudge was an itch that needed to be scratched. What was it that would provide relief, comfort, and an escape for the pain? My decision ultimately led to the biggest wakeup call of my life.

If I didn't grieve properly the first time when Meredith passed, I had no chance the second time with Natalie's death. I wasn't even going to try, and that decision really cost me. I needed an escape, an outlet apart from working. I could have allowed my alcohol consumption to get worse, but then I might have had an accident while driving, or get hauled in for a DUI. It could have been suicide. I couldn't turn to drugs because I knew I'd be dead. I just know my personality – I probably would have jumped over any and every gateway drugs and then fall into the hard stuff so fast it wouldn't have been funny. There was gambling, but I wasn't going to waste my family's income and savings. I never dreamt my landing place would be pornography. That fateful fall of 1997 I found myself curious about this new world to which I had introduced myself.

Had I quit every vice I had in my life and committed to be the best mentally and emotionally healthy person, the best father and best husband I could possibly be, my life could have gone a completely different direction.

*Every person's battle!*

There was a point when I faced that crossroads but I chose the wrong direction because I had found something that offered comfort and gave me the ability to check out of reality yet was pleasurable and best of all, I was the only one who knew about it. My budding addiction hit me at a time when I felt like it was kind of a good place to hover. Then, I hovered too long and afterward, I came clean six years later when I was forced to do so. The best part is that I have been able to stay clean.

I've heard it said, "People don't wake up one day and say, "I think I'll become an alcoholic today. Today's a good day to become an alcoholic." No, you take that first drink and there's a progression. With pornography, it's the first picture you see. The first website you visit. It's a gradual progression of an escape. The numbing effect is just like the right amount of alcohol does for you on a temporary basis... until you do it the next time and the next... all addictions creep up on you – as this one did for me, and before I realized it – my new habit had turned into a full-fledge addiction.

The longer my pornography viewing continued, the lies increased, the acting out behaviors multiplied, and life became more and more unmanageable. Oftentimes with addiction, others can see it, but many times the vulnerable one cannot. Promises of help and healthy interventions are heaped on by those who love us. For the most part, they are acknowledged and pushed aside. Because addiction does not stand still, it inches forward to a predictable ending. Knowing the ugly truth and ensuing consequences are not enough. The ending is the most desperate place on earth, the bottom!

I've been there and it's ugly. You feel like you don't have the ability to get out of it—and you're stuck. You don't think you'll ever be healthy again.

*"Wearing a mask wears you out. 'Faking it' is fatiguing. Keeping up with what you said to*

*who you said it – is an exhausting way. Lying is a hard life for a person to choose. The most exhausting activity is pretending to be what you know you aren't."*

**~ Rick Warren**

To some point, you don't want to stop even if you could. Because I remember thinking, "I could stop this pornography today but I don't *want* to give it up." I was the only one who knew about it. I figured I wasn't hurting anybody. I wasn't spending anybody's money. There were no victims. I told myself all this stuff but I know nothing *made* me turn that computer on. They say it's an addiction, and I believe it, but I tried to live in a way that it was not an addiction because that is a huge crutch. I try to look at it like nobody ever forced me to turn the computer on, ever. I did it every single time and I knew what was going to happen every single time.

I remember sitting there so perplexed and so conflicted. My vices meant that much to me. I didn't want to give it up. That's just crazy thinking. And that's what happens with delusional thinking and cognitive distortions. You convince yourself. I thought it was similar to alcohol or drugs—where you think you can handle it; you can turn it off anytime you want. You trick yourself into thinking you're in total control of your actions.

There are many opportunities in life to experience comfort from pain. They all are based on the idea of getting a quick "high" to make them feel better, even if only for a second. It could be a cheeseburger, ice cream, shopping, hitting a golf ball, taking a hit of cocaine, a horse race or game of blackjack, or porn. Each of these provide a short-term gain or benefit to the one becoming accustomed to the individual high. It's a feel-good decision that may or may not leave any residual discomfort or harm. With porn, I found that short-term gain was always followed by pain, and in my case, long-term and damaging pain. It was the threat of future pain that avoided me in my drive for the next rush.

By carving out small pockets of time, I was able to satisfy my newfound world. In my mind, even with the addition of a new habit, my life seemed manageable and harmless. Other than losing sleep, it was all good. It became easier to return to the computer when everyone had gone to bed. Minutes turned into hours so quickly. Little did I know but through self-deception, I had begun a cycle that would end tragically six years later in my office at Iowa State.

Unfortunately, no matter how beautiful you think the experience is, it quickly wears off. Hangovers and drug withdrawals are two examples. Adrenaline seeking behaviors wear off and then you go to the next thing and the next thing, seeking a greater high. Now, this new world became chasing the rush! When images lost their allure, I moved on to chat rooms.

My deal was hanging out in a chat room where I was typing words to someone else as they were assuming a role or personality. It was the ultimate in mind play and fantasy. I knew the person on the other end of the screen could be anybody, but it didn't matter; male or female wasn't a factor because it was the words that counted. And the words were the fantasy that was played out in my experiences at that time.

Ultimately, it was the unbridled fantasy that locked me in and began my downhill spiral. If I chose a female in their 20's, 30's as the "role" it would be played out accordingly. But once I made the fateful decision to create fantasies with females younger than 18, I was done. One such night, I was involved in a chat. On this critical night, fantasy took a turn for the worse. The person pretending to be a high school girl was in fact a 42-year-old man from Indiana. Why he was playing that role I'll never know, but that matters not. His next move was to call the authorities about the chat and on that night, an investigation began, unbeknownst to me. So much for fantasy; this became real and I was instantly powerless over my upcoming future! My distorted thinking told me, "I'm not hurting anybody—I didn't touch anyone, and I'm not doing anything wrong." That night's chat resulted in a life-changing event; one that would alter my life forever. The chat room wasn't my only legal downfall. During my six-year dance with pornography I obtained and sent images via email. These emails at times contained images of minor females, ages 15-17, across state lines, therefore making it a Federal crime. Though a small number of images were found on my computer, the point is that my demand for receiving and sending images does one thing: it produces victims and proliferates the growth and demand for more websites, images, and video. At Butner, I learned that there is no such thing as a victim-less crime, especially in my case. It's a heavy thought because my actions changed the lives of many, many people; a very sobering thought.

> **"When you've experienced excess, everything else is just bland."**
>
> **~ Nikki Sixx,
> former Motley Crüe bass player**

Looking back, there was an emptiness to me. I thought of myself as a cup that needed to be filled. My attempts to fill the cup with healthy things had been unsuccessful. Someway, somehow, I had to feel better about myself. I felt like I was sinking and the water was up to my chin with no hope of rescue in sight. Filling a cup that can't ever be filled is a losing game. Once the cup drains itself, the urge and excitement, fueled by selfish desires, leads us back for more.

Pornography, alcohol, drugs, gambling, food, shopping, and money are all used to satiate the emptiness in our lives, only to destroy us further and further. Of course, we know these things deep down. Surely, I wasn't addicted to pornography. I always had a choice to stop; but at that time, I just never wanted to make that choice. Instead of fessing up, I chose to run and hide!

> **"Running is futile. You are always chased by one who never tires."**
>
> **~ Randy Brown**

Some believe that the Internet is the primary cause of man's obsession with pornography. I absolutely disagree. We make choices that can pave the way to self-gratification, including porn. The first choice is to turn on the computer. The next issue is recognizing your motive for getting on the web. Internet access takes a second. It is as accessible as the oxygen we breathe. The three A's have allowed much in our world to become the norm. Porn is dangerous for men, women, young, and old because it is Accessible, Acceptable, and most of all, Anonymous. I knew exactly what I was about to do and it wasn't by mistake. In treatment when the word *mistake* was used you were rightly told; "It wasn't a mistake, you meant to look at porn."

How true that statement is.

Only through learning about my massively distorted thinking and beliefs did I later come to realize how wrong I had been. My irrational thoughts, known as cognitive distortions, let me make the bad things seem *okay*. This process of self-justification allowed me to do things others would find reprehensible.

When our minds become deceived, we empower our harmful behaviors by buying into destructive thoughts. When we allow ourselves to believe these irrational thoughts, this process can become our default setting; the way we think determines the way we allow ourselves to behave. We make the inconceivable *okay*.

> **"Sow a thought, reap an action; sow an action, reap a habit; sow a habit, reap a character; sow a character, reap a destiny."**
>
> **~ Stephen R. Covey,**
> ***The 7 Habits of Highly Effective People***

Upon learning about how deeply entrenched my distortions were, I shook my head in disbelief as I admitted to myself that I knew what I was involved in was illegal. This activity was immoral and was being thrown in God's face. I knew Mary Jo was sickened by pornography. I was aware that no one in my life would find my behaviors appropriate. No one except me. I had made everything in darkness acceptable.

If porn hasn't drawn you in or ever become a problem in your or one of your loved ones' life, my hat is off to you.

The danger lies in any choice or behavior that has a negative fallout. Part of the allure of the addiction is to feel power over the night's outcome, or the few minute's risky choice.

It didn't necessarily draw me in as much as I chose to allow it to pull me closer. Once you take that first step and access porn, it becomes habitual, and stopping becomes more difficult. Every day when you turn on the computer with the intention of gaining some pleasure you are building a case for it to be okay. Once it becomes a problem, the floodgates are open and they will hurt you, the victims you view, your family, and anyone else in your life. The obsession can become larger than all of those put together and can only get bigger, unless you make the choice to stop. My thoughts were centered on the fact that I wasn't hurting anyone, it didn't cost money, and no one but me knew about the things I was doing.

*Imaginary Lovers*, a song by the Atlanta Rhythm Section, describes perfectly what awaited me. Every night there was a world inviting me in. Pleasure was always available. Drawn in with perfect bodies and sensuous poses, the temptation heightened. Inside the screen of my laptop existed a world that never said "no"! In that world, it was possible to see anything I desired and say or type anything I wanted within chat rooms. The freedom to express myself with no restrictions brought moments of euphoria to my grief-torn life.

What began as a visual attraction to images soon turned into collecting them. This is called desensitization and can lead to addiction. When someone looks at pornographic material for a period of time, they will become desensitized to the material and may require more variety and more extreme images to find the same satisfaction as they previously felt. When the rush wears off, the person seeks the next level of pleasure. Fortunately, the escalation that I experienced stopped at fantasy, eliminating any face-to-face exposure.

Images provided access at any time. There was always the urge to find an image a little more beautiful than the last. Searching for nirvana is an impossible task but it pulls you along ever so easily. Next, I found the chat rooms I had heard so much about. Clueless at first, I figured out how to find them. All it takes is a fantasy and you are off to the races. More than images and video, I found real time chat invigorating. The invitation is there to play out, or type out, any fantasy you desire.

But, there is no such thing as fantasy unless it's in your own head. Because if you've been on your own on the computer in a chat room, you may think like I did, "If this is my fantasy, I can say anything I want to say."

This is not true.

### Before the bomb dropped...

Thanks to my friendship with Cedar Falls HS Coach, Jerry Slykhuis, I volunteered at Cedar Falls High School over the next year. Slyk loved the game and I enjoyed being on the floor with he and his Tigers. (Tragically, Jerry and his wife, Jane, were killed in an automobile accident on December 20, 2016 near Liberal, Kansas. They are missed by so many.)

At the end of that year, I accepted a job with a friend in North Carolina who had built a successful global sports business. I set up an office in Cedar Falls and dove into a new opportunity. Something held me back, but I appeared to be giving it my best effort.

A trip to Belgium highlighted that work experience, which ended after nine months due to some internal marketing projections with the business. Next came a full-time job as a substitute math teacher at Waterloo East High School. I had previously taught math and found it engaging. Unfortunately, the students didn't.

When the call from Iowa State came, I jumped at the opportunity, leaving the classroom behind.

# Chapter Twelve
## Diet Coke and Championships

The silver lining in the midst of my year off was taking frequent trips to Ames and spending time with Cyclone head coach, Tim Floyd. Based on the amount of time I was around the program I felt more a part of the staff than not. It was a nice diversion from my secret world and the numbness I felt at the time. Tim always took care of me and provided me the gift of staying close to the game. I sat in on staff meetings, stayed at their home, attended practices and games. He even had me run his father/son basketball camp that summer. Our love of fishing was mutual and always led to tales of the next one we'd land. Today, we are fierce competitors on the water.

At Floyd's prompting, I wrote a job description for administrative basketball assistant, which Tim shared with then athletic director, Gene Smith. All he was doing was greasing the skids for me and it worked. A few months later, I became the baton passed from Floyd to Eustachy. In one of my most memorable moments, I sat on the sidelines at their practice prior to their opening round game in the Big 12 Tournament at Kemper Arena. With Floyd, it was a good idea to always pay attention. As I watched, my mind drifted a bit but was jolted by the sound of my name. "Coach Brown, how would you guard the post in this situation?"

"Oh shit," I silently screamed to myself. One minute I'm daydreaming and the next I'm on the floor, telling Tim Floyd and his players how to defend Missouri's 7-1, 300-pound Monte Harge. It taught me to pay close attention at practice!

I was hired as an assistant coach at Iowa State University, where exiting Coach Tim Floyd headed to the Windy City as the Chicago Bulls new head coach. Utah State Coach Larry Eustachy arrived unassumingly in Ames in 1999 and would become the most successful coach in Cyclone history. I was thrilled to jump back into the frying pan and soon reconnected to my passion once again.

As a basketball coach toiling in the national spotlight at Iowa State, I was on top of my game. These were my best years personally in terms of coaching excellence. Our 1999-2000 team won the first Big 12 regular season championship at ISU in 50 years, when Harry S. Truman was President. The only blemishes in our Big 12 record of 14-2 were an overtime loss at Colorado and a double overtime defeat at the hands of the Oklahoma Sooners in Norman. At the Big 12 Post-Season tournament in Kansas City we beat Oklahoma to win the Big 12 Tournament Championship.

We ran through Central Connecticut State and Auburn to advance to the Sweet Sixteen. UCLA was the next victim in an 80-56 blowout. That win pitted us against Tom Izzo's Michigan State team, known as the "Flintstones," because their roster was laden with players from the Flint, Michigan area. The Elite Eight winner would advance to the 2000 Final Four. More than once I thought back to the 20-year-old who set his goals; the third was coaching in the Final Four. This was as close as I would get.

> *"It was the best of times, it was the worst of times."*
>
> **~ Charles Dickens,**
> ***A Tale of Two Cities***

We lost a heartbreaker in front of a home Michigan State crowd in the Palace of Auburn Hills. Following a speechless locker room gathering, I aimlessly wondered the curving hallways of the Palace. I found an open door, stepped inside, and broke down in hysterical crying. The Zamboni I used as a resting spot could have cared less! The Spartans advanced and won the NCAA National Championship. Our 32-5 record was the best in school history as was our modern era Big 12 regular season title and Elite Eight appearance.

The next season looked promising even though we lost our powerful post player, junior Marcus Fizer, to the NBA. Returning was a gritty, tough-minded group along with some freshmen who would quickly make a difference, too. Kantail Horton, Paul Shirley, Martin Rancik, and Jamaal Tinsley represented toughness and winning. Our team captured another regular season Big 12 Title as well as an appearance in the NCAA tournament. Our regular season 13-3 record also included two overtime finishes.

An overtime loss at Oklahoma State and a four-overtime classic in Columbia, Missouri were two of our three losses. Unfortunately, we exited the Big Dance quickly with a first-round loss to Hampton. The exhausted look on our players' faces after that game in Boise, Idaho, said it all. They had given everything the human body was able to give. The 25-6 season made our two-year record an amazing 57-11. No two teams had ever given more. I am so proud to have been involved in coaching them to this unprecedented accomplishment. Little did I know that was the last time I would compete in the NCAA tournament for the rest of my career.

There were other plans in store for me!

Personally, it's fitting that I went out riding a good wave. Will there ever be another Championship run like this one? That remains to be seen. I relish the accomplishments, but more than that, the relationships with the managers, coaches, and players.

The memories and friendships are truly what coaching is all about.

<u>1999-2001 Iowa State Basketball</u>

57-11 Combined Record

27-5 Big 12 Record, four of five road losses in OT+

Won in Phog Allen Fieldhouse back-to-back years; including home games, beat the Jayhawks five games in a row.

16-0 Home Big 12 Record, 11-5 Road Big 12 Record
Back-to-Back Regular Season Championships
2000 Big 12 Tournament Championship
2000 NCAA Elite Eight, 75-64 loss to Michigan State, eventual National Champion
2001 NCAA Tournament appearance, first round loss to Hampton
2000 NBA Draft-Marcus Fizer, 4th pick first round
2001 NBA Draft-Jamaal Tinsley, 27th pick first round
Larry Eustachy, AP National Coach of the Year, 2000
Big 12 Coach of the Year, 2000 & 2001

Larry Eustachy resigned his position at Iowa State in the spring of 2003, just three months after my resignation. He told the world of his addiction to alcohol and admitted he needed help. He offered to step aside to attend to himself and help his family. He boldly stepped into Alcoholics Anonymous to face his demons. The guy with the turtle neck, motorhome, and pop cooler has rebuilt and taken four different NCAA Division I programs to the NCAA tournament. That doesn't happen by accident. A method to his madness, yes. A consistent winner, for sure. The genius of Tim Floyd and Larry Eustachy will forever be preserved within the walls of Hilton Coliseum.

Our world sneers at those who hit bottom and have to ask for help to get back on their feet. Instead of a sneer, each of us should applaud anyone who has the courage to admit weakness, and more importantly, confess on their knees that only the help of others can save them. That's what Larry did and so have millions of others. There is a verse in the Bible, 2 Cor 2:10, that pronounces that when we are weak, we are strong. That is the rock-solid truth!

One of the sad realities of our world is the fascination we have with those down on their luck. Instead of compassion, we joke. Instead of lending a hand, we run. We live in a world that is much too quick to judge. In judging others, we privately make personal statements about ourselves. Do we ridicule and snicker at someone struggling because we have done the same thing? Can we feel better about ourselves if we disassociate with a person in need?

Maybe it's our way of numbing an experience in our past we are not proud of. If there is one flawless person on earth, I haven't met him, yet. If we all strive to be better today than the day before and live by the Golden Rule, it's all good!

Most importantly, instead of looking inside, we assume superiority with a masked face. I'll be the first to say that I'm guilty of judging others, but I also know what it's like to be judged. I truly feel that judgement can only come with people we know well. "How can you judge me if you don't know me," has rattled around in my head for years. Think of friends who have sinned and think about how you responded. I bet you came from a place of compassion and forgiveness. That's why it seems so wrong to cast judgment on those we don't know. Think about this for a bit.

I actually had a guy ask me if the red and white cooler behind the bench was full of Natural Light beer. I looked at this clown and said, "Larry had an addiction and he needed that cooler close to him." The guy was shocked. "Really," he said. I retorted, "Yes and when the game gets tight, he just has to have another caffeine-free Diet Coke!" I went further to explain that he drinks a lot of caffeine-free Diet Coke, just as millions of us do on a daily basis.

Realizing I had a fish on the hook, I told him that if he drank three Coke's or more, our defense and rebounding improved and there was an 87% chance we won at home and an 82% chance we won on the road. The guy was amazed. "You mean you take the cooler on the road too? Did you have the cooler when you played Michigan State?" "Yes," I explained. "In fact, we have a manager named Boji and his one and only job is to prepare ice and guard the cooler, home and away. He sleeps with it." What began as a passive-aggressive slam against Larry ended in another hook, line, and sinker victory.

I will be the first to admit that Larry is his own guy. If he's addicted to anything, it's getting the best out of people. Whether you are a manager, player, secretary, Sports Information Director, or coach, he pushed to max out your potential. The only reason my four years at Iowa State were so fulfilling is not because of the success we experienced. My tenure was all about my development as a coach, from A to Z. Larry pushed me, uncomfortably, many times, into rising above things I had never done before. With a teaspoon of paranoia and a tablespoon of the end of the world, my game sharpened.

A foundation of development and success is being put in situations where you are uncomfortable. Progress comes from being placed in situations you would normally avoid. It's called the path of least resistance, a phrase common in the basketball office. In the moment, I wondered about the truth of the statement. But as I look back, being uncomfortable pushed me through barriers for the first time, coming out on the other side even better.

Our student managerial staff could tell you a few stories. I was in charge of this group, who spent unreal time and effort to do all the things that go unnoticed by the fans. My dilemma was that if one of them did something stupid, which they were known to do at times, the wrath of Larry would come down on me. Therefore, I would transfer his displeasure to the managers. Having had four girls, I now had seven sons to keep in control. We spent a lot of time together and they were outstanding in every way. Knuckleheads for sure, but "shirt off their back" kind of young people. They had an amazing zest for the game, but excelled in the fun factor, making each day a holiday. As a coach, you relish the continuation of friendships beyond basketball and those guys have continued to be special to me. The stories? They will be reserved for an upcoming book, I promise.

## A Double Life

I lived an exhausting double life. Life on top of the college basketball world was incredible. But the guy who wore the suit on the bench was also the masked man away from the floor. Somehow even without much food, too much drink, endless hours working and too few hours with family, traveling for the team, stress and little sleep, I was able to be my best. How was it possible to function at such a high level while living two lives? I have always been able to work on little sleep but this was extreme. When you are involved in living a double life, you just can't do without finding a way to fit them both in. Stubbornly, I held onto a secret way of life that slowly destroyed me from the inside out and way too few knowing the truth at the time.

I handled my outside image well—while inside, I was rotting away like a dead animal on the roadside. I looked fine, but felt dead. Sporting a suit and a determined look, I coached to the best of my abilities before the bright lights of the national limelight.

## The Bomb Drops

On Thursday, January 23rd, 2003, I was busy working on a video tape for my Nebraska scouting report. Pulling together the final edit clips would get me close to wrapping up the report and later that afternoon we would introduce Nebraska's offense and defense to our team. In 48 hours, we would go to battle with Nebraska Cornhuskers.

A knock on the door broke my concentration as two men introduced themselves. I listened as I watched my tape, barely glancing up. I told them to see our secretary Julie. They persisted and again told me who they were and that they wanted to speak to me. The suits were conspicuous and so I finally gave them my attention.

When the door closed and the men asked their first question, my body went into shock. Every nerve ending of my being exploded like fireworks as I sat motionless in my office chair.

They were calm and calculated, just as you would expect from two professional Federal Postal Inspectors. The line of questioning pertained to my online interaction with the man in Indianapolis. If there is a sensation that dwells between shock and freedom, I was there. On one hand, I knew the jig was up and proof of that was that these guys were for real. On the other, I felt my body become lighter as if shedding 50 pounds in the name of freedom; freedom from the bondage in which I had allowed myself to be enslaved.

Frozen in my chair, I stared at my phone as if it were going to jump off the desk. My arm rested nervously on the right arm rest. In my mind, I quickly formed a scenario where the thing to do was to make a call to my attorney for advice and direction on what my next move should be.

I did no such thing.

Should I have made the call? Did I do the right thing? With my eyes on the phone, my arm would not move. I was unable to reach for the call that may have changed my life. It was one of those God moments that is unexplainable. This was the sign to fess up and begin to face the gravity of being caught. The two stoic men finished their questioning, and said they'd be in touch, and left.

Being catapulted in a mental and emotional stupor, I went down to practice and tried to act normal. For the next two days, I tried to act normal. On Saturday, we defeated Nebraska 71-61 though I don't remember one play from that game. On Sunday, I sat down with Larry to fill him in on what might come to light about my life. As expected, he was a rock for me in that moment and offered to do anything he could for me during the process he knew I'd have to endure. His comfort and support will always mean the world to me. Sadly, that Saturday would be the last college game I would coach and the game I now faced was colossal and the odds were against me.

The next 14 months were a blur and a test of my patience and waiting. Just two days after the game, I left for 44 days at a crisis intervention facility in Topeka, Kansas.

After that my days were filled with processing, worrying, and staying busy. Meetings with lawyers were crammed with the unknowns of my situation. Though normal everyday life became a thing of the past, the days became more doable with time. I had my friends, family and faith, and that's all I needed.

I began to attend a 12-step program, dove into therapy, and read voraciously. I filled journals with thoughts and observations about my plight and where God was taking me in all this. In time, I stood in a Federal courtroom awaiting words from the judge that would lead me on an extended "vacation" far, far away. As I began recovery from my addiction I learned many lessons, including how to let go of the grip I allowed pornography to have on me.

The following story is one such lesson that hit home.

African jungle monkeys provide a powerful illustration of the dangers of addiction. A study done years ago attempted to prove that danger was not a mitigating factor to monkeys when it came to their love for bananas. A box was set up in a clearing that served as bait for the monkeys. Bananas were left in the box and only a small round opening was offered. The opening was just big enough for the animal to get his hand through to grab a banana. Eventually the first monkey approached the trap and grabbed a yellow treat. The men stepped into plain site with guns, providing the ultimate danger to the monkey. Even with life in the balance, the monkey gripped the banana tightly. Unfortunately, the monkey didn't realize the treat couldn't be pulled through the opening. Therefore, it decided to hang on for dear life, risking it all.

It could have been the baseball card I had to have but really didn't need. Maybe it was the extra cast I threw into the lily pads to land that huge largemouth bass as the sun set. Possibly, it was the set list taped to the stage I begged for once

' the band left the stage. Was it the Bud Light at closing time? *No*, this time it was the empty, mirage-like pull of pornography. That impulse that promised much, but delivered misery, was what I held onto at that time.

This says everything about the danger I faced during my nights on the web. I ignored the potential risks of my behavior because of my overwhelming desire for the high of porn and my distorted thinking that provided a pathway toward doom. Once I was confronted by the two men who came to my office, and really let the gravity of my situation settle into my spirit, I dove head-first into a deep pool of depression. I discovered that it is the "hidden" malady that affects millions of people. Some are brave enough to reveal their vulnerability and tell people that they suffer with depression. Others suffer in silence, hoping they can somehow mask it with fake smiles and positive self-talk. Both ways, it's there and it's relentless in its pursuit.

# Chapter Thirteen
## Abyss of Depression

*Abyss: "a hole so deep or a space so great that
it cannot be measured."*
**~ Merriam Webster Learner's Dictionary**

Touring Alcatraz Island today is much different than in 1984. Technology now provides a more informational experience. Some people like that approach, but I'll take the 1984 version any day. Both times I visited the island, it brought a chill up my spine that stayed for hours. The realization that the worst of the worst in the United States were harbored in those dingy cells made me shiver. The 1995 Alcatraz experience was more of a high-tech version. Everyone was equipped with headsets as we walked through the prison. During that visit, the movie, *The Rock*, was being filmed, and the doubles for Nicholas Cage and Sean Connery fought right in front of us.

The vibe in 1984 was much different. Clint Eastwood starred in *Escape from Alcatraz* in 1979, and during our trip to the island, everything looked just as the movie did. On that tour, the guide carefully described details of each part of the prison. Parts of the movie would pop into my head as we moved from cell to cafeteria to D block, which housed the worst inmates in five cells that were outfitted with a six-inch thick door void of windows. The three interior walls were also solid. Throughout our tour, the guide recited the names of prisoners who had stayed on D block: Al Capone, Robert Franklin Stroud, the "Birdman of Alcatraz," who inhabited cell 42 for six years, George "Machine Gun" Kelly and Alvin "Creepy" Karpis, who served more time at Alcatraz than any other inmate.

*"And if you gaze long enough into an abyss, the abyss will gaze back into you."*
~ **Friedrich Nietzsche**

Our Alcatraz guide, during the 1984 trip, opened the door and I saw one of the most awful things I'd ever seen. The room was six by six feet with a hole in the floor for urination and excrement in one corner. Food was delivered through a small door that opened and closed. When shut, the cell was void of light. The tour guide asked if anyone would like to step inside the cell for ten seconds. No volunteers stepped forward, so I agreed.

As I stepped inside, I paused momentarily, thinking this may be the end of me. The cell was dark with the door open, but when shut, I was surrounded by the darkest dark I could have ever imagined. The loud thud of the door closing, made me think of how many men had heard that same sound and stood exactly where my feet were planted. I started counting to ten but the smell and darkness quickly overtook me. I reached out and touched the cold walls, imagining a person living day to day in such tiny quarters. After what seemed like 10 minutes, the guide opened the door. Unbelievably, I had survived Alcatraz... but believe me, the memory would last forever.

On that day at Alcatraz in 1984, I thought I had seen darkness, but it wasn't even close to what I would face in the years to come.

## Profile of Depression

Depression is a brain disorder that affects every aspect of a person's life. In most cases, people who are clinically depressed have either lost interest in day-to-day life or feel chronically unhappy, or both. Depression may stem from issues related to brain chemistry, psychological stresses or social anxiety and often gives rise to a wide range of physical symptoms and behavioral issues. Problems related to sleep, appetite, ability to focus and lack of energy are all possible as are thoughts of suicide. A number of famous people from all walks of life have had the disorder. While depression was sometimes seen as a shameful secret until the 1970s, society has since begun discussing depression more openly. Earlier figures were often reluctant to discuss or seek treatment for depression due to social stigma about the condition, or due to ignorance of diagnosis or treatments.

That's the medical view of depression. I've found that each person has a different perspective on what it is and feels like. Some event or thought can trigger depression as if a tap on the shoulder says, "Here I come." I've learned a lot from reading other people's interpretations of the disease. They are in the trenches with me and can really describe the feelings of fog that comes with the territory.

In September 2015, *Des Moines Register* Writer Daniel Finney wrote candidly about his bout with depression and weight control. In fact, his ongoing series on these and other personal topics has allowed readers to get a deeper understanding of the daily struggles of someone afflicted with this disease. "Melancholy is a good day for someone who suffers from depression, however, deep depression is a black, brutal, cancerous thing that erases all hope and turns your mind against itself," Daniel states. "When I struggle with major depression episodes, I hate myself. And I'm using the word 'hate' intentionally. I am completely incapable of feeling good about myself."

Daniel's efforts to find relief from depression are ongoing as he searches for alternative treatments and his articles on describing what depression feels like are amazingly accurate. The cycle he describes has been the same for me.

**"If there is no struggle there is no progress."**
**~ Malcolm X**

I found that a simple trigger set in motion a depressive episode whether I wanted it to or not. The sensation is a flood of melancholy indifference that is so overwhelming, my whole system drowns in it. The body, mind, and emotions are all sabotaged at once. While there is no pain, the combination of all three is a precursor to the emotional depths that will very soon follow. You can try to be the tough guy and rush headlong into the oncoming storm but it won't get you far, or you can curl up in the fetal position and moan your way into slumber.

Through many such episodes, I adopted a process that worked for me. First, I would let my family know how I felt and that I was going upstairs to lie down. We all knew that "lie down" was code for being out of commission for 24-48 hours. My family always asked me if I needed anything and my answer remained the same, "No, thank you." Depression takes over your physical body from head to toe like nothing else. I always wondered if certain drugs accomplished the same deep slumber as depression. The sleep that comes is mandatory and is as deep as anyone could ever hope for and for me, time passes in clumps of four to eight hours at a time, sometimes more. The physical sensation is one of your body sinking into a thick cloud; you feel twice the weight as if you have lost all muscle control. The feeling of being sucked into the bed is heavenly and sleep is instantaneous.

> *"There is no point treating a depressed person*
> *as though she were just feeling sad, saying,*
> *'There now, hang on, you'll get over it.' Sadness*
> *is more or less like a head cold—with patience,*
> *it passes. Depression is like cancer."*
> **~ Barbara Kingsolver, The Bean Trees**

I describe the feeling as a haze in which nothing is in full sharpness of vision; a dense fog surrounds the edges of everything and honing in on an image is difficult. For me, the cycle of sleep and the surrounding depressive side effects were manageable and predictable. Food was out of the question. Instead I drank water. Nothing seemed to speed up or slow down the process. Depression and its side effects controlled my mind and body...and I felt helpless.

To wake up and sit on the bed was victory and to stand up and go to the bathroom was success. Walking down the stairs felt strange but good at the same time. I'd make it downstairs only to get as far as the couch; I'd plunge into it, frozen in a pose. Maybe I'd get up after a couple of minutes and journey back upstairs to go back to bed. If I was up to it, I would step outside and sit in a chair or walk down the driveway but it felt like scaling Mount Everest. At times, I walked around the block, which left me totally wiped out.

I found it difficult to talk to my girls when I was in a depressed state. I could see by the looks on their faces that they were worried about their dad—they just wanted to see their dad well. I wanted desperately for them to understand why I was bedridden but they were too young and didn't know enough about the disease to understand what was happening.

> *"Depression is the most unpleasant thing I have ever experienced.... It is that absence of being able to envisage that you will ever be cheerful again. The absence of hope. That very deadened feeling, which is so very different from feeling sad. Sad hurts but it's a healthy feeling. It is a necessary thing to feel. Depression is very different."*
> ~ **J.K. Rowling,**
> ***Harry Potter* book series**

Unless they have experienced depression personally, friends and family cannot understand what this disorder does to a person. Someone not understanding what depression is all about is the same as me not knowing what OCD, PTSD, ADHD, Parkinson's or dyslexia feels like. I would recommend that loved ones learn about depression, how it works, and adopt practical strategies when it hits. This approach will aid the depressed person as well as those closest to them, including family, friends, and co-workers. Too many times my family walked on eggshells as if I could fall and break like porcelain. I bought a book—complete with yellow highlights and dog-eared pages—about how to live with someone who is depressed. I offered it as an opportunity to learn about the disease, but don't know if it was touched.

At times, others considered my state "convenient," as if such a thing was possible. The message that came across was that I chose to be depressed when I wanted to check out. Nothing could be farther from the truth. It is impossible to expect loved ones to know what to do when depression hits. The answer is usually "nothing."

A couple of years ago, I left our family Christmas celebration upstairs to head downstairs to sleep. I could no longer function and knew that Mr. Depression was alive and well and making a visit. The disease checks in on its own schedule whether we want it to or not. I had read, *When Someone You Love is Depressed: How to Help Your Loved One without Losing Yourself,* and considered it spot on. My hope at the time was that others would read it, too.

If you are suffering from depression, be patient with your family, because they too, are affected, and they don't know what they don't know. Be gentle and patient and take care of yourself. As depression episodes repeat themselves, you may learn the best tactics for handling your loved ones in the best possible way. In time, you'll become an expert on the signs that precede depressive episodes and also the timetable of returning to normal.

There's a story that describes the journey of a man in the depths with no hope in sight.

He started at the top of a hill on a gravel road. Starting out slowly, he worked his way carefully down the hill. Every 50 steps or so an invisible 10 pounds was added to his shoulders. Slowly he was bogged down with 20, 30, and then 60 pounds of weight he didn't offer to carry. At the bottom of the hill he slowly turned over his right shoulder and looked to the top. How beautiful that spot now looked to him. He turned optimistically to begin his journey back up the hill but crashed in a heap. Unable to move, he moaned and cried, "Life is cruel. It's too tough for me." He then curled up on the sandy gravel, unable to move an inch.

# Chapter Fourteen
# I Feel Like a Number

*"One does not expect to be comfortable in prison. As a matter of fact, one's mental suffering is so much greater than any common physical distress that the latter is almost forgotten."*

~ Emmeline Pankhurst,
*My Own Story*

My recurring dream came to visit: Anxiety dominated me as I found myself in prison again. The atmosphere was loud everywhere as inmates rushed to the chow line as if lunch had legs. I remember thinking, "Why would you be in a hurry to eat the worst food of your life?" Frantically I searched for the C.O. in charge of transferring inmates. Surely there had been some kind of mistake. He was nowhere to be found. I sprinted back to my unit and saw some familiar faces, but most of the population was new to me. "Maybe that's how long I've been away from this place," I thought. One thing was for sure, though, I was back in the bowels of prison. I tracked down a guy I knew from my first stay, and he said to go back up to the captain's area at the end of lunch and I would find him there. Suddenly it was time to race back up the hill to find the captain.

Inmates crowded the walkway returning from the chow hall and I felt impatient. I heard insults and warnings to slow down by the angry, angst-filled voices of the guards, but I couldn't stop. I finally got to my destination. There was a long line to see the C.O. in charge. I saw him but couldn't get his attention. I was sweating and my hands were shaking. My fear was if I didn't speak with him, I would be stuck in prison for the second time.

An attempt to cut the line was a bad idea. Turf in prison is measured in inches. I stayed in line as I saw my window of opportunity disappear. As I left the building, others in line followed. I circled back and two officers grabbed at me to go back to the unit. I unwisely shrugged them off and made a beeline for the man in charge. I spoke directly to him, "I'm not supposed to be here," I pleaded. "I did my time and was released. So why am I here? I've got to get home; I have a family and have to support them. I just can't be here again!" The guard looked at me and slowly shook his head. "It's not my decision," he said with an expression as serious as a heart attack. Then I was pulled away by a huge man who looked like a bouncer at the Whiskey A-Go-Go in West Hollywood. I was thrown out the door and walked back alone to my residence. My cell was empty and I lay on the bottom bunk in tears. "Why am I here? There is no way out now and I will probably be here forever!"

The scene faded away as dreams do. This dream is the same every time and is frightening once inside it. When I wake up, I realize I'm in my own bed—in my own home, and prison is a thing of the past. In the past, maybe, but the experience is a part of me forever.

This dream may haunt me now, but during the long span between my arrest and sentencing I had other worries.

———

The process began the moment my secret life was discovered and can be wrapped up in one word: waiting. I waited to go to Menninger's, a mental health facility in Topeka, Kansas; I waited to return home and then I waited to meet with my attorney. I waited and waited and waited.

My longest wait was the period between January 2003 and May 24, 2004. I soaked in as much quality time as I could with my family and friends. My routine consisted of attending individual therapy, marriage counseling and three to four meetings a week, reading constantly. The feeling in the air was cautious at best. For a year and a half, I visualized that 10-second experience in Alcatraz over and over and over.

Time with Claire and Jane was a positive blessing that arose out of the waiting period. We grew very close spending tons of good times together, yet the unspoken was impossible not to hear. "My dad is going to prison," they silently said to themselves. "I don't even know what that means," seven-year-old Jane must have thought.

Honestly, the time spent anticipating prison is worse than prison. The abyss they call prison can be debilitating. So many unknowns, so many unanswered questions. Wonder, worry, wait – for 16 months.

> **"If everything happens for a reason, that means you made the right choice even when it's the wrong choice."**
>
> **~ Lil Treyco**

What seemed like forever to arrive finally descended on us like a blast of artic wind. The sentencing date sucked me in, ready or not. To gather support for my cause, I had solicited 400 family, friends, and colleagues to write to the judge on my behalf.

"My secretary loves her job – especially getting the mail," my lawyer said to me one day while meeting in his office. Missing the point of his statement, I asked the reason. "She loves the letters from all of the coaches and big-time people." I chuckled because he was serious, and it was a laugh of gratitude. I was doing all I knew to do. Gather support and maybe, just maybe, the Judge would go easy on me. It's hard to know if the 313 letters of support helped me, but it certainly didn't damage my efforts.

At Federal sentencing, it was as if Judge Longstaff's lips moved without making a sound. He shot glances at me as he continued to read. The room was deathly silent. I knew what he was saying was nothing more than a legal formality—

federal regulations and statutes—legal jargon that fit the setting just as rebounding, defending, and shooting were part of my world. A verdict was forthcoming and inevitable.

What made this scene different was that it was no Perry Mason re-run on black-and-white television. This was real-life drama, the kind that you never expect to happen to you. The kind you see on CNN while eating popcorn on the couch. This time it was different; this time it was me. On this day, in April 2004, I was the one who rose when the defendant was asked to do so.

> *"Prison is a second-by-second assault on the soul, a day-to-day degradation of the self, an oppressive steel and brick umbrella that transforms seconds into hours and hours into days."*
> ~ **Mumia Abu-Jamal,**
> **The New Penguin Dictionary of Modern**
> **Quotations**

I slowly stood, locking my knees into place. Looking the part of a well-respected citizen, I was decked out in the suit that had seen tight games won and lost to Kansas, Michigan State, Duke, Kentucky, and UCLA. This time the stakes weren't losing or winning a basketball game. I was saying goodbye to what I'd previously known to be my life. Even with all my realities, I somehow still felt composed and amazingly in control.

Heightened fear and shock will do that to a person. Dozens of family and friends figuratively held me up as I faced the judge eye-to-eye. I remembered a scene from fifth grade when I stood before my imposing elementary school principal, scared stiff, and shaking like a leaf. Although my nerves were steady in court that day, the consequences were much greater than school ever dished out. Instead of writing, "I will not mock the teacher" 100 times, a different kind of punishment awaited me.

In what seemed like endless babble, much of which I didn't follow, the judge paused, looked at me, and said that the decision was out of his hands. *I guess that means it's out of my hands too, then*, I thought. Because of mandatory federal sentencing, my prison term would follow those guidelines regardless of any sentiments the judge had.

I was being treated as well as could be expected but it didn't really register. I was too frozen to realize the situation was going as it was supposed to go. The legal rhetoric came to an end when the judge announced a prison sentence of "24 months." Motionless and emotionless, I heard the message as if Ken Sawyer, my junior high football coach had screamed it from a bull horn. Twenty-four months...two years...anyone could do two years...but in prison–PRISON? If the sentence length was an uppercut, the sudden rush of reality, of prison, was the knockout punch.

————

Instantly, nausea set in while the blood drained from my head. My eyes remained glued to the judge as he said the unthinkable words of, "24 months." When he asked if I understood, I offered a simple nod, a weak "yes," and then he told me to sit down. My back remained stiff and as straight as a private in basic training. I turned to my right and met the eyes of my lawyer, Tim McCarthy. My mind raced like traffic down the 405 in Los Angeles, speeding out of control.

*You've got to be shittin' me*, I thought to myself. *This can't be happening. How does a guy get put in prison for two years by looking at pictures on the Internet? Surely this must be a mistake; we can get out of this, can't we?*

The shuffling of papers by Judge Longstaff signaled the end of the court session but the beginning of a different kind of adventure. Sitting in that second story courtroom in downtown Des Moines, I suddenly and sadly realized my life had changed forever. Here I was lifeless, yet fully conscious of what had just happened. It would take a while to sink in. For all but two days during my 16-month wait for my day in court, I believed that prison was not an option. Maybe out of protection, Tim had shielded me from this reality. Every second that passed added to the weight of reality.

I slowly turned around and stared into Mary Jo's eyes. The hurt I saw there was indescribable. Then I looked at my mom, dad, sister, and brothers—what pain and embarrassment I had caused them. I had gone from big-time college basketball coach to sex offender and felon. *What's happened to my life*, I thought.

## Pretend Jail

*The Andy Griffith Show* stands out as one of the greatest entertainment values ever. A person can't help but laugh at the antics of Andy, the sheriff of Mayberry, and his trusty sidekick Barney Fife. I grew up on that show and continue to watch it to this day. The show gave me my first glimpse of jail. In that tiny Mayberry sheriff's office, the cells were rarely used. As Barney exclaimed many times, these cells are only for "the most incorrigible criminals" like Ernest T. Bass or the town drunk, Otis Campbell. Maybe I laughed at those episodes because I felt I would never be in jail. Prison is for bad people; criminals who make their living breaking the law.

## Pre-preparing for Prison

While waiting in Ames, I took a friend up on an odd offer. How would I like to visit a prison? A friend had volunteered for Chuck Colson's InnerChange Freedom Initiative prison program and visited the State prison in Newton monthly. I quickly agreed to go with him but I'm not exactly sure why. The trip to Newton wound me into a ball of nerves. Why would I ever want to spend one more second in prison when I had two years ahead of me? The intimidating visit went without incident. I wanted to take the edge off the constant picture in my mind of the sights and smells of my future home. Seeing the men in Newton gave me some confidence that, although I was not like them, I could exist with them. Only time would tell what my real prison experience would reveal.

Having received many calls from friends of friends who had been in prison, I decided to meet with one man at a mutual friend's house. He filled me in on the life I would grow to accept. He was helpful but bitter about the situation that led him to an eight-year term. He no longer acknowledged the American flag, blaming the government for his misfortune. Like any good coach, I gathered information as if I was recruiting a hot prospect again. In this case the prospect was a federal facility tucked into the thick forests 22 miles northeast of Durham and Chapel Hill, North Carolina; the hotbed of college basketball. How ironic!

My dad got a call from a local acquaintance who had served time for a white-collar crime a few years earlier. I was encouraged to call him and hear his views on how to survive prison. It was then that the word "survive" took residence in my vocabulary. The visual and sensory perception of what *surviving* might mean was sickening. He did say to my dad, "Tell him he will have a life in prison." That comment conjured up all kinds of possibilities; most were acceptable at best. What could this mean? Unaware at the time of the validity of his statement, I could only sit, worry, and wonder what *kind* of a life my future might bring.

## The Waiting Game

In the end, because I had broken the law, I had to pay the penalty. All the blaming, justifying and rationalization in the world wouldn't help. Facts are facts and I was going to prison. A voice echoed in the far-reaching hallways of my brain. The inner voice wanted to know what happened to my life and why this was happening. It spoke constantly to me, repeating the plea heard from all men who hit bottom, "How in the hell did I get here?"

The final weeks before prison were the worst because there were so many unknowns! Where would I be sent and when? Five weeks after sentencing, Tim McCarthy called. I had been thinking that I would be placed in a camp, the kind of relaxed prison setting that others I knew had experienced. I was hoping for a camp assignment in South Dakota or in Rochester, Minnesota. I spent way too much time trying to plan and justify things completely out of my control.

Just before I went to prison, a friend introduced me to ✗ Viktor Frankl's book, *Man's Search for Meaning*. Frankl describes in chilling detail the life of a Jewish prisoner in the Nazi concentration camps. It's required reading for anyone who thinks life has dealt him or her a raw deal. Frankl stood naked in freezing weather without food, was psychologically, mentally, and emotionally abused, but he somehow survived. He explains in the book that the human mind is incredibly resilient. What we can perceive, he says, we can do. He proved that.

Frankl shares that a person's attitude is the one thing that cannot be taken away from him. Not the military, not terrorists, not Mother Nature, not even Hitler and his men could defeat the inner mindset. Not surprisingly, I re-read Frankl's legendary book shortly after arriving in prison. I took it to heart and used his insights to exist in my own prison.

In the months that I waited for my facility assignment, the descriptions of his experiences were my constant companions. Thinking I would be placed into a camp or at worst, a low-security prison helped a bit. That bubble would soon burst.

Because of the judge's recommendation, I was assigned to the medium-security Federal Correctional Institution in Butner, North Carolina. I say "assigned" because men are sent to this treatment facility via requests from judges from all over the country. Actually, the men of the SOTP, Sex Offender Treatment Program, in Butner are some of the most fortunate prisoners anywhere. Located within the confines of a medium-security compound, the SOTP unit is self-contained and serves as an intense, no BS 24/7 treatment facility. Only 100 men inhabit the unit, leaving over 10,000 convicted sex offenders on a waiting list to toil in harsh settings, without treatment, all over the country. Little did I realize at the time how fortunate I was to be sent to Butner. What resulted was another gift of God's game plan to surround me with great people as I had been in previous years, from coaches to friends to unlikely strangers.

Of Butner, my lawyer said, "It's a top-notch program and you'll be able to work on yourself." My head nodded "yes," but my mind said "no". Besides, North Carolina is so far away from Ames, Iowa. In addition, I had to come to terms with letting go of the idea of a camp setting and accepting the reality of entering a medium-security prison. I approached this new information much like a youngster who reluctantly carries a D-laden report card to his parents.

Quickly, we put our heads together and began to plan. My attorney warned that even though I was to self-surrender in North Carolina on my own, the quicker I could leave the state the better.

"Why?" I asked.

"Because the prosecutor wants you taken into custody now and transported to prison," he replied; "I advise you to go, and go now!"

———

Wow, what an adrenaline rush in those final hours! I went from receiving my assignment to being informed that I was on the loose and could be taken into custody at any time. I felt like a fugitive who needed to escape the scene before the Feds caught up with him. Basically, the Judge did me a favor by allowing me to surrender myself; much to the displeasure of the authorities.

As I packed my bags and took one last look at my home, my Dad declared, "I'm driving you out there; no exceptions." On the fly, my brother Roger jumped in, too, sacrificing days at work simply to aid me. The comfort of traveling with them all the way to North Carolina cannot be overstated; a real gift of love and support.

In all the excitement and commotion, I hadn't even thought of how I'd get there. I just knew I had a day, May 24, by 9:00 a.m. EST, to report to Butner. Feeling like I was in an adventure movie, I left my home within 20 minutes. The house was filled with family and friends, and we relocated quickly to the other side of town. Tom and Jane Jorgensen's home on quiet White Oak Drive became our "ground zero." The Jorgensen family has been a life raft of support since 1984. They are real people who care more for others than anyone I've known. I traveled across town with friend, Jeff Rutter. Jeff drove cautiously down the streets of Ames and through the university to avoid traffic. Not wanting to even see a police car, thinking they would stop us at any time... ran over and over in my head.

———

Once at the Jorgensen home, we gathered in their front room and Uncle Tom played the piano to lighten the tension. Tom, a liver transplant survivor was special to thousands of people; a true gift. Tom died while I was away on September 7, 2005. I said my goodbyes to everyone except Mary Jo and the girls. The four of us convened in a back room, held hands, and said a prayer. As my kids would tell me later, it was a "long, long, long prayer." My last hugs with them were next to the car that was headed east shortly. My heart was not prepared for the devastation of those last tears and hugs. Dazed, I climbed into the back seat of my dad's van, waved goodbye and took off.

My dad, along with my brothers and I, have probably made more fishing trips together than most people have been to McDonald's. It had the look of yet another bass trip, but the mood this time was different. I don't remember much about the trip other than talking very little. I began reading, *Bringing Down the House*, a book describing the MIT students who scammed Vegas casinos for millions. The risky and daring adventure allowed me to escape if only for a minute at a time. In the two years to come, I would covet time reading books for purposes of escaping the mundane life of prison.

Staring aimlessly out the window as we zipped through the Smokey Mountains, I wondered, "How much pain have I inflicted on my family?" Rog and Dad had quickly and unconditionally volunteered to get me to Butner as if it was some routine daily decision.

"Do I lean on a wedge or smooth a nine," Rog may ask himself on the golf course on an average day. "Grapefruit or cereal," my dad may wonder. There are common daily choices, but to decide to drive your son to North Carolina, and to prison no less, was anything but average. "How about leaving now and driving 1300 miles to check Randy into federal prison for two years?" *No brainer; let's go.*

———

The power and unspoken force behind unconditional family love is a true wonder. I couldn't have asked for a better family or childhood. My sister, Renee, was the youngest, and had to deal with three older brothers every day. Yet, with all of that going for me, I used others to satisfy myself and hit the bottom rung on the ladder. With family and many friends behind me, I headed toward the unthinkable. My decision and life choices determined my path. In a few days, all physical signs of my former life would disappear, and I would be faced with one of life's toughest opponents.

They say that a man in prison has a choice. He can learn to be a better criminal or a better person. I chose the latter. As I soon discovered, this choice was not as easy as selecting AC/DC instead of Kansas to listen to on the stereo. With my decision came a full commitment to do whatever it took to make the changes needed in my life. I certainly didn't want to become a better criminal; I knew that much. "Heck, I'm not even a criminal to start with," I mumbled. "I'm so different than the average guy who's in prison; not even close." I would learn in the next 21 months how wrong that thought was.

At 5:30 a.m. the alarm went off in the Holiday Inn room in Durham. As the significance of the day hit me, my stomach knotted up. It stayed that way for several days to come. The day was May 24, 2004, D-Day! Instead of buzzing over to Duke a few miles away to hunt down Coach K or visit Roy at UNC, I headed in a different direction. Eating was out of the question so coffee won out. My normally weak desire to eat at all had completely disappeared.

I don't remember much about that morning. I just knew I had to check into Butner at 9:00 a.m. We headed north away from Cameron Indoor Stadium and the Dean Dome on the way to Butner. Tucked back in the woods, the town could be renamed Heartbreak City. Littered with nearly a dozen prison facilities, the small town sat and waited for me. After two misses, we found the right place. Once we finally arrived, it all hit me. "Federal Correctional Institution," the sign screamed at me.

A weird sensation came over me as I noticed an American flag proudly displayed atop the flag pole. For years, starting in elementary school, where we recited the Pledge of Allegiance with pride every morning, I had revered the stars and stripes. As a basketball player, I would count the stars on the flag during the national anthem. It was my pre-game ritual to curb nervousness. Now that same flag represented something awful – justice and the strong penalties imposed on all lawbreakers. This same flag was now as threatening as any symbol known to me. As I made the gruesome, slow walk to the front doors and the inevitable, I could vaguely hear those famous words from the Black Sox scandal of 1919, "Say it ain't so, Joe!"

At the front desk, I identified myself and said I was there to self-surrender. This was a big deal to me. The tightness in my stomach was worse than any Featherstone Park induced hangover from my youth. "Okay... now, what did you say, who are you, anyway?" boomed the barrel-chested officer. At that moment, I realized how true Bob Seger's lyrics are in his song, "I Feel Like a Number," because I was now a number, #06828030. Many times, in the coming months, I would circle the dirt/cinder track of the rec yard here, listening to Seger's words. How true they expressed what I had learned to fear...I feel like a number!

––––––

"Sit down" was the impersonal command. Speechless, the three of us took our seats. I looked at my dad's face and it brought tears to my eyes. The lines on the 76-year-old face spoke of anger, fear, and sadness. Suddenly, it was as if I could hear his thoughts, 'My son is going to prison.' Caught somewhere between a whimper and a full-blown outburst of tears, I hung on. Rog slapped my knee a few times to keep me steady. Unspoken gestures stirred heart ripping feelings in the depths of my soul. Nothing was said. Without a doubt, this was the most frightening and uncomfortable family moment ever. I felt young and helpless and vulnerable. My heart begged me to grab my dad's leg, crying, "No, Daddy, don't let them take me away, please, Daddy!" I was 46 on the outside but only seven on the inside.

> *"After one has been in prison, it is the small things that one appreciates: being able to take a walk whenever one wants, going into a shop and buying a newspaper, speaking or choosing to remain silent. The simple act of being able to control one's person."*
> **~ Nelson Mandela**

For the first time, I heard the dreaded sounds of jangling keys, a sound that would dance in my head for two years every second of the day. Officers passed to and fro in the reception area. *Some reception*, I thought.

The next words I heard will always haunt me. "You can go now," the officer said stoically to my dad and brother, his voice breaking the intense silence my family and I were enduring. Not knowing what to do, we stood, looked straight into each other's eyes, and hugged and cried. I can't begin to explain the avalanche of emotions and confusion at this time. In a second they were gone. I sat down slowly, wishing I could call my family back for just one more hug and "I love you," but they were really gone.

Now, I stood alone within the confines of my new environment, but it was just another cookie cutter day in the Bureau of Prisons (BOP). I was soon told something that was hard for me to swallow: "You're different from everyone else in the world. You're different. You're a felon." How does a person deal with such a truth? It's a truth that stabs through you like a frozen blast of a North Dakota wind.

I learned later that my dad and my brother Rog left immediately and drove straight home in one long shot. Roger returned to work on Tuesday and Dad watched Jane play soccer the next afternoon in Ames. I can't imagine how surreal it must have been for him to watch his son's daughter that day.

Self-surrender is what the authorities call it when you give yourself up. Not only did I dismiss the idea of prison, but I imagined that if it ever did happen, it would go the same way that it does in the movies. The blocks were cold, drab, and impenetrable. But I'll take concrete to bars anytime.

In the end, the Feds wanted to take me in movie style but the judge's movie recommendation won out. I, Randall Alan Brown, would self-surrender my freedom and the life previously known to me. There's not much to it, really. You simply walk into your appointed facility and say, "I'm here." From there, in precision and brilliance, the BOP takes over your life.

In the past, I've been described as organized, efficient, and calculated. The treatment staff at Butner chose words such as smooth, slick, manipulative, and coercive to describe me. But they were in charge and I was just another broken-down inmate.

The word that I chose to adopt as my anchor was *perspective*. How I viewed this experience was what would determine the scope and depth of my stay in prison. I have always been a positive, forward-moving person but I was about to be severely tested. Not only have I leaned on the positive in the past, I am built to believe much is possible if a person wants it badly enough. I've seen little in my life that I couldn't attain. "It requires a game plan, preparation, creativity and a ton of hard work, but it can be done," has been my personal motto. If kept in check, this can be a valuable part of someone's character.

## Treatment

Feeling like a human research project, I entered the voluntary treatment. How does a person remain positive in the face of the horrors that awaited? It came down to a choice. We choose how we see our lives, the direction and the circumstances that litter our paths. I also chose the behaviors that got me to where I was.

During treatment at Butner, I would say that I "stumbled across" a particular website and the world-class doctors on staff would go crazy when they heard "stumbled upon." They would say, "No, you didn't stumble upon it, you *meant* to find that website." And they're right. The words the doctors can pick apart are incredible. They were so good. I was taught the language of responsibility when I was in treatment because our words say everything about what we actually mean about something. Was I really responsible for that happening? I was... kind of... early on my choice of words inferred the computer was at fault, the tragedies in my life caused my actions, or what I had done was a fantasy and harmless. I would learn that how I formed each sentence would signify my willingness to accept responsibility. They taught me to use my words in a way that reflected the truth.

I need to tell you that a positive outlook and the urge to vomit do not happily coexist. Shock would best describe my first minutes in prison as I was being processed by the officer. One thing I learned in prison was to refrain from asking why. Why? Why? Why? Why not ask why? Because you'll never get the answer you want, and the answers you get makes no sense. I repeat, no sense.

Friends and family tended to ask a lot of questions about my experience in their effort to make sure I was safe. Shortly after asking my first 100 "why" questions, I figured it out. Don't ask; just do. I had to come to terms with the fact that my situation was nothing like what my life was like on a normal day at home. Though normal had not honestly been a part of my life for some time now. Yet, I realized a 'normal' day in my new surroundings would need to become clearer for me to survive.

Prison is not a Democracy. I had to train Mary Jo, and my constant visitor, childhood buddy, Bart Warren, not to fall into the *why trap*. All common sense goes out the window as you play by only one set of rules. Whether they make any sense or not does not matter. I heard it said that the Feds can move third base any time they wish, especially after you've rounded second base.

I learned quickly to shut up and do whatever I was told. God has many methods of teaching us. He knew I needed humility in my life but chose a funny way to supply it. Sitting in a cell that was bare except for one worn out cot-like bunk bed and one metal desk, I waited. The sound of lead dead bolts sliding into place were frightening.

As I studied the concrete, my mind went blank. All the anticipation of safety, sanitation and noise was about to be answered. All I could do was hope for the best. Minutes into my first day, I sat in a holding cell, waiting to be processed and assigned to a unit. The cell was bare. Once they brought me out of the cell, they took my photo and handed me my very own fire-engine red ID card. *The guy on my ID looks bad*, I thought.

A medic checked a few things, and I was taken through my first of many humiliating and character building strip searches.

Next, I followed the medic to my destination. Instead of walking shoulder-to-shoulder with the burly man dressed in blue medical scrubs, I lagged behind. Instantly, I felt inferior. "You going to Maryland?" he uttered. "I'm not sure," I replied. Those were the only words he spoke, and I later learned that was routine. To be sure, a requirement in prison is the ability to mind read. Oh, I could tell you some stories. At the end of this 90-second journey, the medic pointed at one of the units and said, "Over there." I was able to bond with my first staff member on my first day here; we were tight! As I drew close to the Maryland unit, I could feel the glare of many sets of eyes. Like the new kid at school on his first day, I became the rookie in the unit and last on the list.

The unit I walked into resembled nothing like what I expected. It was orderly. *Okay so far*, I thought. I stood in a hallway, frozen and lost. The guard guided me toward my check-in with the CO (correctional officer), who mumbled something about B-Pod, room one.... His words did not connect but I somehow found my room, 130. There were no bars; in fact, the cell even had a door. The walls were concrete blocks, just like in the movies. I met my 'cellie', which is prison lingo for 'roommate', and then was greeted by many inmates in the unit. Their handshakes and greetings seemed genuine. Obviously, this treatment program was a little different from the images of prison I had conjured up in my mind.

My cellie began to ask the usual questions. "Where are you from? First time in prison? How long you been down? Do you smoke?" Fortunately, my first cellmate looked and behaved normally. I expected a lot worse. In fact, I had to laugh inside, because he was the spitting image of a hometown friend B.J.

Once his questions were behind me, I began to take in the seemingly endless litany of rules I would have to obey each day. Overwhelmed at first, I began to commit names and faces to memory. I kept a pen (a good assistant always has a pen) and paper stuffed in my pocket and made notes as needed. "John, from Cleveland, 40ish, drives an 18-wheeler, loves to fish the big lake."

I got a kick out of seeing the looks on faces the next few days as I greeted inmates by their name. Usually it took weeks or months to perfect, but I was trained in the art of notetaking. Recruiting 300 players for four roster spots will do that. Some habits are etched pretty deeply into me, and note taking was one of them. Quickly, I learned that suspicion rose as I jotted down details so I learned to do it on the fly.

Ahead of me lay a steep learning curve, however, I took it all in—with the true will to succeed, even here. I quickly discovered where the bathrooms were, because I was sick. My first three days I felt as if I would purge my entire digestive system at any time. I experienced dry heaves but of a different sort than I had known in the past. The heaves physically illustrated in detail how I felt inside.

Faces, handshaking, and rule after rule is all I remember from that first long day on May 24, 2004. My first night in prison I cried enough to grow Iowa corn. It was a deep and hollow feeling like nothing I had never felt before. And this was just my first night with 604 such nights to follow.

Within the fences of prison, I learned that patience is indeed a virtue. A person who can't exercise patience, perspective, tolerance, and non-judgment will go insane in prison. Your insides will be eaten up slowly at first, but over time, it will consume you completely. All that's left is the outer shell of a man with cold, indifferent eyes and a heart that is empty. I made a commitment not to become that man. Unfortunately, prison is full of these men whose similar intentions have been slowly eaten out of them, revealing a landscape of the living dead. They are lonely, cold, and tired. No white flags of surrender are needed because the inmates' blank faces speak for them just fine.

I might as well have been at Disneyworld on a crowded sun-drenched summer day—everywhere I turned, there was a line; for food, the bathroom, the drinking fountain. Prison is the Disneyworld of those whose lives have gone wrong.

Prison is one of those places that most of us never dream will be a part of our personal reality. We put it on the list of things we'll never experience in our lives: being a millionaire, winning a Nobel Prize or an Oscar, becoming a rock star, spending time in prison. Just like you, I kept this list in my head, too. Yet, as I wrote these words, my location set me apart from 99 percent of you.

# Chapter Fifteen
## A World Within a World

*"After all, even in prison, a man can be quite free. His soul can be free. His personality can be untroubled. He can be at peace."*
### ~ Oscar Wilde

It was just another Saturday at Butner. I peered onto the court from behind a stone cold two-foot by two-foot metal pillar. With one eye closed, I studied the play before me. Background noise filled my head and made me feel nauseated. I wondered what was worse—the constant barrage of noise and profanity or the quality of play on the basketball court. One team finally won the turnover-ridden game.

I rarely watched fellow inmates play, but today it helped me pass a little time before the "move" (a "move" is when the guards signal that it's time for inmates to get from one place to another. Like from the track to the unit for example). In prison, five minutes can seem like five hours if you allow time to be a constant focus. One strategy is to always have a book handy to read. Even if it is just for two minutes, the words in that book catapulted me into the story and out of the prison, temporarily. I also kept records of my daily walking by recording the day, time, duration of walking, laps walked, distance, and steps taken. If you know about the book, "The Slight Edge," you can appreciate how these numbers grew by a small amount, day by day. Over time, the numbers soared and gave me a real sense of accomplishment. After studying a map, I decided my walking goal would be Denver. I felt that in two years, if I walked every day, I could walk the equivalent of 1690 miles. I posted that number in my locker and was motivated to reach the mile-high city. A strange thing happened: I got to Denver in 15 months. I had nothing else to do so I just kept walking.

I had created a daily discipline of exercise and stayed with it every day. No less than 6 days were missed out of 605. My routine was this; the mail call was at 4:00 p.m. each day. At about 4:20 the move allowed me to get to the 1/3-mile track and begin the day's journey. My strides were bold and confident as I usually walked alone. In 78 minutes, I could cover 18 laps which was 6 miles. Weather was not a deterrent; but, during the winter my socks became gloves and my towel was my head dress. I burned through three pair of Adidas running shoes. That left about 5 minutes before the next move. All in all. I walked 2222 miles, 6666 laps, and 5.2 million steps. Exercise was my best friend every afternoon. The trip ended somewhere in the middle of Utah!

My weight progressively dropped to the point one of the doctors asked about my health. My size 34 pants were loose as my lowest weight hit 169 pounds. An induced weight loss plan I suppose, but it worked for me. I don't think I could even drive to Utah today!

Any activity that would keep my mind from the negative was a worthy use of time. I learned quickly how to be creative with my mind and engage in activities inside the razor wire of prison. A loud buzzer signaled us to move while inmates were released like cattle on a Kansas ranch, all destined for the next lonely spot.

At 9:18 p.m. that night, as I lay on my taco-shaped cot, I heard voices approaching. The COs were conducting the mindless job of counting inmates. God forbid someone would escape. The count was a nightly ritual and was just a major part of being in the prison world. I uttered a monotonous, "Brown 06828030," as I focused on the background to avoid eye contact with the officer. I stood at attention with my cellie until the last inmate was accounted for.

I hated that six-minute wait each night. My enemies of fear, suffering, anger, and disbelief attacked my head and heart from all angles. It was the longest six minutes of the day for sure. The "all clear" was the elixir that helped me relax and plot the rest of the evening.

Behind bars, the noise never ever stops. You can count on two things never leaving this God-forsaken world: hopelessness and noise. Both were a part of my life at Butner every single day. Once horizontal, I stared at the wall from the top bunk. By now I knew every intricate detail of the concrete mass. Poured in slabs and absent of any esthetic appeal, the wall signified the life of an inmate. Nowhere to go. Not up, down, right, or left.

### *"The hardest prison to escape is your mind."*
### ~ Unknown

One particular night, the wall seemed to draw closer to my face, moving one-tenth of an inch every minute until the feeling became overwhelming. I jumped to the floor and splashed cold water on my face. I resumed my spot a few minutes later. *What a relief*, I thought as I exhaled a massive cleansing breath.

I heard a loud voice just outside the cell—probably just another senseless brawl between two meatheads with nothing to do. I'd become impervious to such nocturnal encounters. Quickly the guards broke it up and a profanity-laced war ensued for about half a minute.

My head sunk just two inches into what they called a pillow. Truth be known, it was more like a cotton wafer that had been wet and dried in the sun every day since the prison's inception. "The Marriott this ain't," I muttered. Becoming immune to the noise, I drifted off to sleep without setting my wristwatch alarm. A dream abruptly awakened me, causing me to wake with a sweat on my brow. "What happened? Where am I," I asked myself. The answer deflated me.

My thoughts returned to the pick-up basketball game I had witnessed earlier in the day. I remembered the constant screaming and arguing that was as commonplace as the net on the rim. They all wanted the ball. They all wanted to shoot. The inmates all wanted to show what they could do in a game that none of them could play. And not one of them played with passion. It hit me hard! Prison ball reflects how we all got here. It's a game played without accountability. It's sloppy without a hint of execution or pride in the effort. Complaining and arguments serve as shields to the truth both in the game and in life. One made shot and life is great. But get your pocket picked, and you embarrassingly come up with another victim-motivated excuse. In the prison pick-up game, no one is ever at fault. Entitlement is as thick as the criminal record of most of its players. As I pondered these things, the daily question zapped me: *How the hell did I get here?* With that, I fell back into sleep with no memory of the prior brief dream that had awakened me.

> *"The whole value of solitude depends upon oneself; it may be a sanctuary or a prison, a haven of repose or a place of punishment, a heaven or a hell, as we ourselves make it."*
> ~ **John Lubbock**

At 5:00 a.m. a person in prison can actually find some solitude free of noise. My habit was to set the alarm on my watch to get up at that time each morning, even on weekends. A small pocket of sanity is worth beating the crack of dawn. Step one every day was to fill my cup with water and instant coffee and set the microwave. I could do it blindfolded like every other mundane task. Step two was to crack open my Bible and have my devotional time for the day. Surely the Lord above loved me and was keeping me safe. Maintaining my strength and faith was a full-time chore in this hell hole. I wrote hundreds of notes in the margins of my Bible and God spoke to me quietly each morning, putting his own special spin on the words and verses. I jotted down most of them for future encouragement. I had no colored highlighters or fancy pens. I was allowed one pen and one pencil although I found a small purple colored pencil under a table in the chow hall. I carefully used this prized possession but of course it dwindled in size each day. To sharpen it, I rubbed the pencil against rough concrete, shrinking its size a little each time.

The day I walked into this place one thing struck me as being very wrong. They did the unthinkable; they took my Bible. My Bible! "It's not a bazooka," I had silently muttered. "It's the word of God. Are you kiddin' me?!"

Although it took some doing, two weeks into my stay... I talked the chaplain into giving me a standard NIV version Bible. The overworked servant of God had more requests and complaints than he could handle. His supply of Bibles was meager, but somehow, on this day, he forked one over to me. It became a journal of sorts as I loaded the top, bottom, and side margins full of notes as lightning bolt thoughts came in the morning quiet.

I marveled at the fact that I could be disciplined enough to get up early and slow life down each morning in this barren place. It was on my list of things I would continue to do once I regained my freedom. My devotional time gave me perspective and tranquility in spite of all the noise and uncertainty of my days.

# Chapter Sixteen
# The Back of the Quilt

"These pains and troubles here are like the
type that printers set. When we look at them,
we see them backwards, and they seem to
have no meaning. But up there, when the
Lord God prints out our life to come, we will
find they make splendid reading."
                    ~ Martin Luther (1483-1546)

Basketball coaches often teach the whole-part-whole method. The idea is to show your team what the "whole" looks like. For example, half-court, man-to-man defense—by breaking down the whole into parts, each role is taught independently. Once the pieces have been explained and drilled, the whole is again presented to the team. Because of the detail spent on each piece, the second "whole" starts to shed some clarity on the defense.

Great coaches understand that concepts are taught from one vantage point, the coach's. Each teaching point is being seen and heard from 15 different individuals with varying learning styles, listening abilities and basketball IQs. The most brilliant coaches I've known are able to coach through their players' eyes. On one level, the concepts must have been seen, heard, and understood. But on a higher-level, players must see how each part fits into the whole without leaving one part out.

## Back of the Quilt on the Court

Precision execution comes from the synergy exhibited when all five players can both "know and do" on the floor. They must play in concert with each other and flow as one unit. The movie *Hoosiers* provides an idea of how coaches convey this philosophy to their teams. Coach Norman Dale, played by Gene Hackman, gives his team an emotional pre-game talk saying, "Five players on the floor functioning as one single unit: team, team, team—no one more important than the other."

> **"God makes all the pieces of our lives fit together."**
> **~ Andrew C. Schroer**

Basketball success comes from each player doing his part, whether large or small, for the combined effort of the team. The team is truly a sum of its parts.

Often, during the process, there can be confusion and frustration from coaches and players. One player cuts right when he should have cut left. Passes are thrown but not caught. Poor vision keeps a defender from seeing the ball penetrated from behind him for a lay-up. All but one player hears the directions coming from the coach. The effort of each player can vary, and that makes the entire unit vulnerable.

Real coaching happens on the practice floor. The pieces can look unsightly at times and coaches must stop, go back, explain, and then do it again. Sometimes, no matter how many pieces you get right, 15 minutes later, all of them have been forgotten. The greatest frustration for a coach comes at this crucial time of teaching. If these pieces of the defensive foundation are not firmly taught and learned early in the season, the dam will leak for the entire season. Therein lies the difference between winning and average defensive teams. To add to the job, understand that half-court defense is just one of the dozens of bigger pieces that need to be performed in unison as a team takes the floor.

Experienced coaches have learned to "see the forest through the trees." They believe in a process that involves careful planning, detail, and patience. When a proven system has consistently been successful, it's much easier to trust the process than rely on the day-to-day ups and downs of coaching a team. Winning comes from a process-driven organization. The focus is on the implementation of the parts once each piece is taught. This process requires having the faith to know in the end that a successful team will be the result. When winning is the only goal, all the things that contribute to continued success may be sacrificed along the way. The wrong aspects of the game are emphasized and the foundational aspects are lost.

With every new college basketball season, you can spot programs that do not maximize their recent successes in order to build even more successes. I truly believe that a poor program that takes years to rise into national importance can be proud of their effort. But as much blood, guts, patience, and luck as it takes to make the ascent, it's much more difficult to stay at that level of winning.

> *"The most important lesson that I have learned is to trust God in every circumstance. Lots of times we go through different trials and following God's plan seems like it doesn't make any sense at all. God is always in control and he will never leave us."*
>
> **~ Allyson Felix**
> ***Living Life on the Back of the Quilt***

I once read about quilt making. The front of the quilt as a finished product is a beautiful, creative work of art. The back is a collection of mismatched colors and fragments that dangle at will and resemble the finger painting of a kindergartener. Once the backing of the quilt covers up the back side, the messy parts are hidden from view.

This hit me right between the eyes as an analogy for how God works in our lives, and it has helped me in times when I struggled to trust God. God is the author of both the front and back sides of the tapestry that is our lives. God creates the beauty but also the rough edges that become part of the final quilt. How else can we make sense of the messes in our lives? We may not always agree with God's responses or the ways He brings about the changes that build the final picture.

Let's look at a perfect example that you may be able to relate to in some way. I'll use fictitious names for the purpose of the story. Let's say Bob and Suzanne's marriage is thrown off by financial difficulties that, in turn, creates a seemingly insurmountable hardship. Hidden below the surface are contributing relational, sexual and communication thorns that have caused distance for both. God is in the details and knows that in the end the difficulty can become a blessing to the couple. Bob and Suzanne get financial counseling and learn steps they can take to begin resolving their money woes. Instituting the advice of their counselor, they create a budget and cut spending. Bob and Suzanne agree to unite in their efforts to make their situation work and they are successful. Their marriage grows closer and stronger as they work together to conquer the obstacle presented. They both look back and see why the struggle was good for them and agree they are in much better shape because of it.

> *"One of my favorite pictures of God's working in our lives, especially during hard times, is the picture of God weaving a beautiful tapestry together with both light and dark colors (joyful and sorrowful times). On this side of heaven, though, we stand behind the tapestry and usually see only the knotted ends and frayed edges of what God is doing. If we could get "on the other side" of the tapestry, we could see God doing something beautiful, but we live on the underside with painful circumstances and God's purposes unclear."*
> ~ **Growing Small Leadership Resources and Ideas, www.southwood.org**

Our quilt analogy applies perfectly to Bob and Suzanne's story. When adversity hit, the financial obstacle became the cause of escalating stress and fights at home. When the counselor firmly told them that they must change their ways, the couple became angry. Bob and Suzanne could only see the back of the quilt—not only their financial woes but also the ugliness that was lurking just below the surface of day-to-day life—and that was a mess! If Bob and Suzanne didn't rally together and change their philosophy and habits around money and other issues, they would continue to live at the back of the quilt. Their amazing transformation allowed them to walk around to the front of the quilt, which presented a beautiful pattern of bright colors and a design that was breathtaking. Their lives, which had been headed for disaster, blossomed into a warm, rich, and nurturing relationship for many years to come.

Quilts are often made from scraps of cloth that are anything but modern day works of art. Old t-shirts, shorts, dress shirts, dresses, curtains, sheets, and even jeans, are cut into smaller pieces and sewn together in different patterns. I remember watching my grandmother intently sew the ugly, odd-shaped scraps together into small squares. I said to myself, "This quilt is going to be ugly with all those pieces of cloth being used." But then I watched as colorful shapes and patterns began to come to life. By the time my grandmother finished with one of her creations, the quilt had been transformed into a tapestry of beauty, fitting together perfectly.

## Standing Strong When You're Hanging on by a Thread

I've heard the quilt referred to as the tapestry of our lives; mismatched, frayed, and messy from the back. God sees the front side, and He's proud of His workmanship, His beautiful creation. He has carefully designed each moment in our lives, especially the significant ones that are represented in the quilt's design. Thousands of experiences are meshed together to make a kaleidoscope of colors into our life's design.

God loves the back side as much as the front. To Him, each loose thread or tied-off piece of yardage signifies starting over.

We must stand tall and create our quilts in the most difficult of moments, knowing that in the end, beauty will be on display. We can find peace by trusting that God is in charge of both sides of the quilt. Increasing our faith allows us to experience less stress and worry, and we can use our faith every day to help us deal with whatever life brings.

"How did I get here?" I've uttered that question many times as I've weaved in and out of the peaks and valleys of this up and down crazy life. I've said it in locker rooms, offices, used car lots, prison, attorney's offices, bars, unemployment lines, searching for porn on the Internet, in the courtroom, and while cleaning filthy prison toilets. Yes, things can look pretty ugly at times, but with faith we will see the purpose behind our knots, frayed edges, and tangled threads.

# Chapter Seventeen
## You Can't Come Back if You Don't Get Up!

*"Every saint has a past and every sinner has a future."*

~ Oscar Wilde

The virtues of friendship are unparalleled. When knocked to the mat it's tough to get up on our own. We need someone there to encourage us, help us, or simply yell at us to "get up!"

We received a special handwritten letter after we lost Natalie in 1998. It came from a very special young man from Lagos, Nigeria. Solomon Ayinla was a junior on the North Dakota basketball team during my one year in Grand Forks. He had a championship smile, an infectious attitude, and a huge heart. His letter said it all; "Get up and get going."

*Dear Mr. and Mrs. Brown,*

*From the word for today. Get up and get going!*

*Regardless of what tripped you, allow God's power to lift you today and put you back on your feet again. We have to learn to react to adversity like yeast when the heat is on, it rises. God will set you in uncomfortable places so you can rise. The bad times often do more to strengthen us than all our mountaintop experiences put together.*

*So, you fell again! Get up again!*

*I will share a part of my life with you, because I know how you feel. We have been trying to have children for seven years, and I don't love my wife one % less, rather I love her more. I know you love Mrs. Brown more; give her a kiss for me.*

*Get up and get going!*
*Solomon Ayinla*

Clichés are for Hallmark cards. The truth is no matter where it comes from, you must get up! You may have to dig deeper than at any time in your life, but you must muster the courage and strength to get up off the mat in the 12th round. Solomon's message has stayed with me ever since the day I received his letter.

If I know anything, I know you can overcome adversity and come out a better person on the other end. You can do it, you were meant to do it. You will need to learn to cry, you will have to learn to get help, you will have to learn to commit to health, both mental and physical. Become vulnerable, weak, and without answers. You can do this but it won't happen magically. You can't want it to happen, you must be intentional for true change; this is a serious undertaking. If none of that works, think of Adam Sandler in *Waterboy*, yelling "You can do it!"

Giving up isn't on the menu. It's not an option anymore. Giving up is never the right choice. Find a way to find the freedom you deserve.

A perfect Bible verse for gaining the perspective you will need comes from 2 Corinthians 4:7-10 (NIV):

*7 But we have this treasure in jars of clay to show that this all-surpassing power is from God and not from us. 8 We are hard-pressed on every side, but not crushed; perplexed, but not in despair; 9 persecuted, but not abandoned; struck down, but not destroyed. 10 We always carry around in our body the death of Jesus, so that the life of Jesus may also be revealed in our body. 11 For we who are alive are always being given over to death for Jesus' sake, so that his life may also be revealed in our mortal body. 12 So then, death is at work in us, but life is at work in you.*

If you lose your job, you are not crushed.

If your marriage fails, be not in despair.

If you are told that you are not good enough, smart enough, or pretty enough, you are not abandoned.

When your finances tank, you are not destroyed.

When health news is too much to handle, with help you will persevere.

No matter what happens, you can pull through it or manage to do it!

## The Final Descent

In the last few years of our marriage, as Mary Jo and I became increasingly distant, we talked about what was going on with us and our marriage because we no longer felt close. Tragedy had pushed us further away instead of closer. I remember telling her on multiple occasions, "I think we are doing really well for what we've been through. I think any expert would say, 'I can't believe you're married because of the statistics surrounding losing a child, let alone losing a second, public humiliation, and imprisonment' is nil."

How could we expect to have a healthy great thriving marriage? We both wanted that, "But I don't think that's realistic," I told her. There was now a divide between us and when you're in survival mode for so long, I just don't think you say, "Okay, I want a happy life now. Let's have a happy life now." Sure, there was counseling, individual and couple, a marriage retreat, books, and lots of soul searching. I did a lot of damage to our relationship with my selfish behaviors. But the load we both carried was backbreaking and apparently, we looked at the last chapter of our lives differently. My wife and I were like a fragile tree branch, weighted down by wet snow and ready to snap at any moment. Maybe we were bound to break.

You could search forever, but you'd be hard-pressed to find a woman more loving and supportive than my wife of 32 years, Mary Jo. It's heart breaking. On the flipside, our divorce represents another loss and failure in my life, one I was not in favor of. I believe there is always a chance to reconcile, but as they say, it takes two to tango. Repeated loss can dampen the future but I'm resolved to make each day a new opportunity to love and be loved. It starts with loving myself!

Tragedy, much less double tragedy, wears on you and a husband and a wife both deal with grief and stress differently. You both deal with grief and loss differently. Stress, grief, and loss are major life stressors and the statistics are just numbers; they don't equate into real life and dealing with the real issues.

During all the separation and divorce proceedings, Mary Jo told me that it was at Miami of Ohio when she first felt a disconnect between the two of us. She was right, because after Meredith's death, I was halfway checked out emotionally and mentally. I always mustered up enough energy for my job, sometimes putting on a mask to make it work. When "they" say, "You'll never be the same," it's true – you'll never be the same. Not to say that is a bad thing, but you're different. You just are.

———

## Marriage in Prison

When I was at Butner Prison, there were about 100 guys in my unit at any given time. Thank goodness that the judge sent me to North Carolina to the only Federal Sex Offender program within the BOP (Bureau of Prisons). Toward the end of my term, there were three of us still married, but one guy was close to divorce. So, the guys there were either single or divorced; three of us were still hanging onto what was left of our marriages. It was hard to see so many guys who were served divorce papers in prison. I started to think about what Mary Jo had endured; that she had really stood by me when most of these people's spouses had abandoned their mate or been unable to wait until time healed their lives more. I thought that was amazing, or, at least Mary Jo and I still being married was amazing.

## A Change of Wind

Little did I know at the time, but every handwritten letter I sent home from prison painted a fantasy of life to come. I wrote letters from Butner that were hopeful and honest, anticipating my return to be a better me with a better marriage and a better life.

Those letters were penned in the most hopeless place on the planet. While many inmates were planning their next crime, I sat in corners and wrote. Writing was a relief and an amazing exercise in pouring the best out of me. In prison, the reason you write to a spouse – is to make the day you arrive home the best one ever. A fresh start where everything will be different, improved and more hopeful. But as happiness became dampened at home, I learned that the sunshine and hope behind my correspondence had not been met with the same hopefulness by Mary Jo. Also, my writing the letters meant so much to me I was not honestly paying attention to see if the mood and hopefulness was being reciprocated.

I wouldn't change a thing in terms of sending hopeful letters home. They came from an honest part of my heart. Who doesn't want better? In trying to do the right thing, though, I was actually setting myself up for the end of our marriage. The world I painted was not the world that waited for me.

The middle of June has always had significance in my life. It was on June 16, 1984, that we were married. My in-laws, Dick and Jean Jorgensen, shared the same anniversary date, which made it a doubly special day. Fast forward to Tuesday, June 16, 2015, the day before my wife nervously told me of a therapist appointment she had scheduled the following day and said that it would be a good idea for me to attend. My suspicion was that her scheduled appointment wouldn't be pleasant, but I went with her. Once we sat down, she proceeded to announce that we needed to take a break from our marriage and have some time apart. I wasn't shocked, and there was a ring of finality to her words.

Mary Jo and I had not previously talked about taking a break from our marriage. In fact, our inability to engage in healthy communication had been a major issue in our marriage. Obviously, her decision was something that she and those closest to her had been planning for a while. She calmly stated the reasons for the meeting, her feelings, what she wanted from the future and what the next steps were going to be as far as her life was concerned. Sure, I knew that we had grown apart in our marriage, but I also felt that anyone who weathered the storm for 31 years deserved our best shot. We agreed to disagree on that point. I still saw a lot of promise and did not want to end our marriage under any circumstances. I had no doubt that if we agreed to work hard in unison on our marriage—it could be salvaged, and the thought of divorce sickened me. Her perspective was much different. She saw our marriage as a void of hope and believed that any amount of work on it was fruitless.

The math is easy to understand. Two people are in a marriage. If both stay committed, the marriage is intact. However, if one of the two parties decide to end the relationship, it's over! Our marriage was over.

It's hard to say how all of the heartache, betrayal, prison time, and lost children affected our marriage over that 31-year period. No doubt it caused a heavy burden for both of us, our parents, family, and friends. So much of what happened on the tragedy ledger had been lost in a fog of tears and shock. There are periods of time I cannot recall at all. I can't remember the voices, the touch or hugs my girls offered me. How could anyone gauge the effect of prison on a marriage? How does the collegiate coaching profession factor into the health of a marriage? I can say that seven moves to six states took a toll, especially given that each was a result of my goal of becoming a Division I head basketball coach. Once I arrived at this hard-fought destination, I wasn't sure if all the toiling represented enough gain.

Our 32nd wedding anniversary was on Thursday, June 16, 2016. We had not lived together for almost a year and rarely communicated. Sounds familiar, right? Four days later our divorce was final.

Losing your mate of 32 years causes a mixed bag of emotions. Not being at all in favor of our divorce evoked immediate anger in me. Truthfully, some of it made sense and, yet, at the same time it didn't. I'm not a quitter so it didn't feel right to hear that our marriage was not working. The sadness at times was and still is heavy. We spent a long time with one another and built a family together. We won, we lost, we grieved, and we avoided. Our marriage wasn't healthy, nor are many others. Life was not designed to be perfect, nor is it. How does someone determine when there is no hope? *There is always a chance*, I thought. The truth is, I may never know.

My wife was a warrior and an unrelenting supporter of mine. I could not ask for anyone better to share my years. Yes, we had our differences and struggles at home, but she worked tirelessly to raise our kids and to be the best at her job outside the home. Mary Jo took pride in providing a clean home filled with warmth. She demonstrated a fighting spirit in her constant trips to visit me in prison. How did she really feel bringing Jane and Claire into that environment to see Dad? It must have been awful... and, I have to remember that. The letters and visits represented her true support and love for me. A gift that few will ever know!

There are definitely some regrets on my end. I hurt a lot of people, especially the ones I loved the most. There is nothing I can do about that now but live to be the best person I can possibly be and be a father to my two daughters and help them through the struggles and celebrations of their young lives. I have so much to be thankful for and am convinced that God has the best act of the play yet to come.

*"There is something beautiful about a blank canvas, the nothingness of the beginning that is so simple and breathtakingly pure. It's the*

> **paint that changes its meaning and the hand
> that creates the story."**
> ~ **Piper Payne**

## Learning from the Birds

Living on your own following divorce provides plenty of time to think and reflect on the past. On a windy winter day while working at the used car lot at Ames Ford, the north wind cut through the sky with a vengeance. On the power lines high above the lot, I noticed a line of birds. There were probably 50 of them seemingly enjoying the cold, blustery afternoon in early December. I turned to Google to quench my curiosity. I learned that birds sit on power lines, trees, roofs, or any perch, facing into the wind. Any other direction would ruffle their feathers and make communication impossible. That's why they face the same direction while sitting. *Brilliant*, I thought; *I'll never look at birds the same way again.*

What I discovered next inspired me and is a perfect metaphor for confronting adversity, bird-style. Eagles love storms. When clouds gather and wind rushes, an eagle uses the storm's winds to lift them higher and they rise above the clouds. Rising above the clouds gives the eagle an opportunity to glide and rest its wings. In the meantime, all the other birds have their own advantageous game plan. When smaller birds fly into the wind, they sometimes don't have to flap quite so hard because the wind is creating lift. They still have to propel themselves forward to make progress or they become like leaves in the wind. By flapping their wings, they fan the air behind them in an expedient manner.

We can learn from the behaviors of eagles and common birds and use the storms of life to rise to greater heights. In large part, I feel a newness; a chance to truly start the next journey. As I embark on this new journey at age 59, I'm praying for headwinds. Just like a flying bird, I feel free. I want to soar higher and higher, knowing that <u>by sharing my difficulties</u>

with others I'm helping as God wants me to. He gives us struggles to use so we can come beside those who also suffer. I'm tired of running from pain. The pain of running away outdoes the pain itself. Facing pain and dealing with the depths of its origin is more difficult temporarily, but pays off down the road. Flying with the wind is easier. Easier isn't necessarily better. Easier is soft, and soft gets you beat. Not only is heading into the wind difficult, but it's good for me. So, I say, "Blow wind, blow!"

> *"You can't start the next chapter of your life if you keep rereading the last one."*
> *~ Unknown*

## 20 vs 59

The only thing I remember about being 20 is the recklessness and pure optimism that guided each day. "Every day's a holiday and every meal's a banquet," my pal Bart used to say. Everything was ahead of me. My NBA playing career had crashed earlier, but coaching was very attractive to me. I ran hard with the group, grabbing doses of music, Butler 3-on-3, and plenty of cold biverds. The freedom available at that age is intoxicating. There is fear of the future but also unbridled optimism in the moment.

At 59, things are different from the way they were 39 years ago. But one thing will never change: I have hope, I have passion and I want to help people. I know I am a good person and can have a positive effect on others. I want to live, not for myself, but for the good of the world. There is pain in the world that sits idle. If my message can help, I want to share it as often as possible. I want to prepare myself to meet my maker face-to-face. I'll have a few questions but I imagine He'll be in control of the conversation.

**New Game Plan**

My home is a personal Rock 'n Roll Hall of Fame. My Marantz amp can pump screaming guitars through my Bose speakers at any time of the day or night. I can plan my day in solitude and have total control of my time. At times, it's quiet, too quiet. I can become lonely and sad although I won't cave to depression and its evils. One of my proudest personal accomplishments is my sobriety and I'll do my best to maintain this. Being able to plan my personal and professional schedule is freeing. Day by day there is light ahead and I'm so excited about what God has in store for me. As long as I stay out of my own way, I'll be able to see the amazing game plan that has been constructed for me and those in my life.

It is true that a lost opportunity will manifest itself and become something greater. My friend Herman Richter, Provost at the University of Okoboji, says, "When God closes a door, He opens up a window." The end is the beginning, and the beginning is the end. The future cannot be predicted so paying attention is of the utmost importance. Be present and capture opportunity when it appears. Stop and look around. There's a chance that every road is going to bring you back around. Be ready!

> *"So, what do we do? Anything. Something. So long as we just don't sit there. If we screw it up, start over. Try something else. If we wait until we've satisfied all the uncertainties, it may be too late."*
>
> **~ Lee Iacocca**

There are still a multitude of things that I need to get done. My message is one that people need to hear and I want public speaking to lead the way for me to reach others. Many ideas that will someday become books currently fill my file folders. My message can speak to someone in the front row or the back row who deals with the same struggles as I did. I'm turning my mess into my message! ~ *great approach*

I want to have an impact on the quality of basketball coaching. We have a game that is precious yet vulnerable. The integrity of the game is a must, showing reverence to all of the great coaches and players who came before us. The game can be preserved with coach certification being the next chapter. Personally, I feel that sweatsuits, pullovers, and shirts without ties should be left at home. To preserve the game's integrity, coats and ties should be standard attire. It's a simple way to show how much the game is respected. Some coaches still get it but many have gone casual, which I think is a mistake.

Most importantly, I have family to connect with and two daughters to guide, support and encourage. Claire and Jane deserve my best and I definitely want to be a supportive and encouraging part of their lives. The future holds very exciting things for both of them and I will be there to celebrate with them.

I will drive an RV across the country and follow my football Hawkeyes at home and on the road in the fall. There are many largemouth bass to catch and release. If I ever learn how to play my Fender Strat, we'll probably have to bring the band back together. As Mick Jagger said, "I know it's only rock and roll, but I like it."

Besides, all I ever wanted to do was play at the Holiday Inn lounge on weekends. I think an acoustic version of "Cat Scratch Fever" would be a hit!

# Chapter Eighteen
# How Do You Measure Up? 15 Skills to Master

So, how do you position yourself to handle a quick-hitting tragedy best? Here are fifteen preventative efforts that can save you much heartache down the road.

## Respond vs. React

Jumping to conclusions may be America's favorite form of exercise. Many say that the way to handle adversity lies in your reaction to it. I disagree. I would replace reaction with a response. Practicing this can be a daily exercise whenever a test comes in the form of a small, insignificant issue, or something heavier. Imagine receiving an annual review at your workplace. As you read it your face becomes increasingly redder. You shake your head as each point of your review is revealed. Before the end of the document, you storm into the boss's office. I do not recommend this approach.

I've found that it's best to step back and use the time to change out the anger and defensiveness for a more mature approach. Switch your point of view and you will find wisdom. Ask yourself, "How could these comments have validity? See it through your boss' eyes, not yours. Take a healthier perspective and consider a comprehensive approach. Time and perspective will act as allies, allowing you to appropriately respond to the issue, not react to it.

## Acceptance

Acceptance has always been a struggle for me. Not until a friend introduced me to the AA definition, did I begin to embrace it. Since then it's been easier. The biggest impact on my understanding of acceptance was my two-year stay at Butner Federal Prison in North Carolina. In prison, you can think you are the angel and the rest of the population are slime balls. Truthfully, that was my thought when I entered Butner in the spring of 2004. If so, I must have looked silly in an angel costume as I cleaned vile inmate showers, urinals, and toilets for 4 hours every morning.

A month into my stay I began to see myself the same as the rest, and that allowed me to accept my fellow inmates whose decisions had put them in the same hell hole where I resided.

It was in federal prison that someone sent me a card with this definition of acceptance:

"And acceptance is the answer to all my problems today. When I am disturbed it is because I find some person, place, thing, or situation — some fact of my life — unacceptable to me, and I can find no serenity until I accept that person, place, thing, or situation as being exactly the way it is supposed to be at this moment."

*"Nothing, absolutely nothing, happens in God's world by mistake. Until I could accept my alcoholism, I could not stay sober; unless I accept life completely on life's terms, I cannot be happy. I need to concentrate not so much on what needs to be changed in the world as on what needs to be changed in me and my attitudes."*

*~ The Big Book of Alcoholics Anonymous*

## The Uncontrollables

I admire those who can differentiate between things they can control and those they can't. That is another area of struggle for me, but fortunately, my time of addiction recovery has strengthened this ability.

> **"My attitude is that if you push me towards
> something that you think is a weakness, then I
> will turn that perceived weakness into a
> strength."**
>
> ~ **Michael Jordan**

I'm always amazed at people's fascination with the weather and food. For many people those two topics make up 90% of their conversation. The weather is a good example of something we cannot change. No matter how many rain dances we do, we see no evidence of water from the sky. Mother Nature has things under control so fussing over it is futile. The stock market, other people's opinions, sports, world tragedies, our health, famines, tsunamis, and hundreds more make up things that are out of our control. The issue comes when those situations cause us to fret, worry, and feel frustrated. Actually, about all we can control is our attitude and approach to life. Everything else, no matter how we try, is out of our hands.

"The Serenity Prayer" has served me well in my recovery. It addresses the control issue perfectly and can become part of your everyday life. It has helped me tremendously through thick and thin. *"God, grant me the serenity to accept the things I cannot change, the courage to change the things I can and the wisdom to know the difference."*

Adversity is out of our control and should be left at that.

## Weakness vs. Strength

It can be a real stretch to see weakness as strength. Men, in particular, are raised in a world that teaches toughness over weakness. When difficult times hit, men want to stay strong as if this approach can solve the situation. Humility, wisdom, and the ability to become vulnerable, to feel the hurt, are the keys to recovering from life's devastating losses.

Two Bible verses address this and explain how weakness is indeed strength: 2 Corinthians 12:10, Paul's thorn and God's grace, reads: *"That is why, for Christ's sake, I delight in weaknesses, in insults, in hardships, in persecutions, in difficulties. For when I am weak, then I am strong."* Philippines 4:13 states: *"I can do all things through Christ who strengthens me."* Notice the verse does not say, "I can do all things, period." That would put the attention on us, not God. We cannot do all things... unless we are humble and surrender all to God. We can become strong through Him because He gives us strength!

## Better, Not Bitter

One of the first sympathy cards we received after Meredith's death brought a strong message. It was early in the grieving process, but the point hit home. Still in shock, angry and, yes, a little bitter, I found it hard to relate to the following sentiment. However, as time elapsed, I understood how toxic bitterness could be. It is an evil root that devours and destroys. The card read:

*The BITTER Choice: Events that happen to us in life create periods of struggle. No matter how earth-shattering our lives are... at the moment... the stark reality is that time stops for no one.*

*Not only can we become stuck in bitterness, but it can also create profound problems for the rest of our lives. Don't be one of those negative people who always connects the quality of his or her life to something that happens as a part of life. You don't want to be that person and others certainly don't want to spend time with Mr. or Mrs. Negative. Now is the time to take the bull by the horns. Be better, not bitter!*

---

*The BETTER Choice: Better is a choice. Strength is a choice. Perspective is a choice as is how we decide to treat others. Refuse to be bitter because joy is something you can choose, and it can transform your life. This is where adversity can offer a path to strength, resilience, and growth. It is preparation for the next challenging life event that occurs. It's easy to see how this works in sports. What if a baseball player got bitter and quit every time he struck out? In reality, a good professional hitter doesn't get a hit seven times out of ten, but the player doesn't suddenly decide to leave the game. Instead, baseball/softball players learn from their strike outs and get better next time they come up to the plate. In life, we have to do the same. If we don't decide to become better, we shouldn't expect anyone else to make it happen.*

## Humility

Adversity offers us an opportunity to take a snapshot of our lives to examine ourselves. Weakness helps us see that we are not as high and mighty as we might think. We are frail and vulnerable, and at times, helpless. As a coach, I've experienced times when I thought the world revolved around me. Our teams were winning and people were patting me on the back at every turn. My confidence was skyrocketing... with no end in sight. All it took was a bad defeat to bring me crashing back down to earth. Humility is essential in our lives. It can aid or destroy your relationships and your career depending upon how you choose to adopt humility in your life.

Stevie Ray Vaughan is known for his guitar-playing prowess. If he had not died in 1990 in a helicopter crash — who knows where his playing would have taken him. Leaving Alpine Valley Music Theater in East Troy, Wisconsin, after a show with Eric Clapton, his aircraft failed to clear the hill after takeoff, claiming the lives of five people, Vaughan included. Stevie Ray has been a mystery ever since, as many are who die young. His playing was off the charts, but in studying his life, videos, and books, I've learned of his tender and humble heart.

Two stories will stay with me forever. First, in a rare interview with a young Stevie Ray, he was asked about his playing ability. The interviewer said, "They say you are one of the greatest guitar players of all time." Stevie replied, "I keep trying to be, I don't know that I am, I just know that I do the best I can." Notice he says: "trying to be," meaning that he didn't feel he was there yet! The answer was not canned as many are. Based on his facial expressions he was clearly showing true humility and giving a sincere answer.

The second example is a reflection he shared on stage nightly after gaining his sobriety. "But there comes a day when you have to come home from the party, you know, 'cause if you don't, what happens is you forget about all the people who love you with all their might. And you keep running from them because you can't look 'em in the eye."

## Grief

I'm no expert on grief although I've taken on my share. Grief is not a choice but at times we must face it. The one dynamic that my marriage never mastered was shared grief. My wife and I were both grieving the losses of our children, but not together. I think this makes a monumental difference. They say that grief can bring couples closer or drive a wedge between them. We chose the latter. My wife's support and ability to cope came from her close friends and family and started immediately after reality set in for her. For me, grief was something I could intellectually understand and talk about but not something I chose to express.

My answer to being ripped apart by mortality was to separate from it. I thought that if I could distance myself in mind, body, and heart, then I wouldn't have to deal with it each day. Those first few days were all about being numb. But as time marched ahead, I faced a fork in the road. One road led to full acknowledgment and acceptance of my beautiful daughters' deaths. This was the healthy choice with lifelong rewards. The other road was darker and narrower. It didn't look like a choice anyone would make, but my feet were stuck in the ruts that led to the darkness. I sought out anything that helped with the pain. Unfortunately, I chose longer hours at the office and film room, alcohol, music, recruiting trips, time on the road with our team, and any alone time I could muster.

Running from grief is like running from terror. You know at some point you have to face the monster but only when all else has failed. Avoidance, seeking pleasure, and escape became important parts of my day and continued until that fateful day in January 2003. Grief will catch you earlier or later — the choice is yours.

The day you run and hide is the day you take your first step to giving up. Have you ever buried something without properly dealing with it? Bad choice! Even toxins buried deep underground will surface. At any time, they can reappear, and it will be a real mess.

> *"Looking back, it seems to me*
> *All the grief that had to be*
> *Left me when the pain was o'er*
> *Stronger than I was before.*
> *And by every hurt and blow*
> *Suffered in the long-ago,*
> *I can face the world today*
> *In a bigger, kinder way.*
> *Pleasure doesn't make the man;*
> *Life requires a sterner plan.*
> *He who never knows a care*
> *Never knows what he can bear."*

**~ Unknown**

Choose the fix now. When your car is running poorly, you repair it. You can choose to let it go but the damage to your engine will be major down the road. Fix *you* now!

## Forgiveness

Forgiveness was not an issue for me during the dark times. There was no one at fault. No drunk driver had ended my child's life, leaving years of tug-o-war inside my heart. In the case of a drunk driver or other negligent circumstance, forgiveness becomes a major part of life. For me, it was anger. I was so angry with God and continued to be for several years. So many people threw out clichés like, "Things happen for a reason." Although meant in good will, that adage enraged me. People use such tired statements because they just want you to know they care. Sometimes the words they use are meaningless, but it is the heart and thought that counts.

Learning to forgive God was a chore. Neither Meredith, nor Natalie deserved to be cut short, but God allowed it to happen for both of my daughters. He didn't cause their deaths, but I believe He allowed it. Each death caused me to be so angry! In time, along with a lot of self-examination and faith-based living, I learned to accept their deaths and stopped blaming God. It took a while, but forgiveness happened.

## Second Chances

They say America is the land of second chances. I'm highly skeptical of that statement these days. Judgments in our world are made in an instant and are often based on what someone does—rather than who they are. Instead of human beings who made poor decisions, people who have made mistakes are considered low-lives, scumbags, villains, out-laws, criminals, predators, and a long line of other derogatory things.

None of this helps the person who is honestly working to make a run at a better life, free from crime, substance abuse and poor choices. Unfortunately, our world sees things differently. Anyone who fills out a job application will find a section for felons. Just the fact that this question appears on the application proves the employer wants to know who is or isn't worthy of a second chance. Being backed into the corner is a certain rejection for many. Are there great stories every day about people being given second chances? Yes, of course. The truth, though, indicates a trend toward employers *covering their ass* before bringing on "one of those people." Most everyone deserves a second chance as long as they are sincere about making healthier decisions and a better life.

## Gratitude

The truth is that no matter what's been taken away, there is always something left. For those who are fortunate, there is a bounty of goodness left. This is simply a case of seeing the whole picture in the midst of loss. Good health, friends, family, a home, job, belongings, and a hopeful attitude are all things we may have to look forward to, and by the way, *no*, it doesn't fill the hole of loss, but it is there to comfort us during the journey, and we can be grateful for that!

## Faith

I see two kinds of faith: intellectual faith and walking faith. A person can be in a Bible studies group, go to church, volunteer, and appear to be a *man of faith*, which could be true. But many people have intellectual faith. They do what seems to be right in public, but the mind, not the heart, is in charge. True faith is about surrender and being teachable.

My good friend, David Staff, the pastor of Christ Community Church, in Ames, Iowa, has a heart for Christ. Before I left for prison he spent hours with me, preparing my heart for the years ahead. He promised to write me every day. Every day? I thought surely this promise would fall away over time. But he wrote every day for two years without fail. This is a man who walks his faith and serves others but is not without humility and sin. He is a true warrior of faith and one who has taught me that God is the answer. He is right. I just need to take his coaching, get it on the floor and execute it in my life consistently.

## Sense of Humor

I've thought many times that God has to be looking down on me and laughing hysterically. When I'm frustrated in traffic, angry about a loss, or venting at Him because my team lost a game, I know He sees the humor in it all. On earth, it's hard to laugh about such things, but the idea of not sweating the small stuff has its merits for sure. Coach Lute Olson, my boss at the University of Arizona, told me once that nothing is as good as it seems, and nothing is as bad as it seems, either. If you think on that for a while, you'll find the wisdom. We need to laugh at ourselves and others. Laughter is good medicine and says to us, "Be good to yourself, you are a super person who can make poor choices, but in the end, don't forget to laugh."

## Selflessness

The pity party always starts with me. Use adversity to realize that others are involved in your grief, too. There is continually an opportunity to help others, which I've always thought was part of the circle of life. We are all in need at some point. Someone out there could use a pat on the back and a cheerful word. If it's not about me, that means it must be about someone else! A good way to dig a hole deeper is to think only of yourself. A way out is to lift someone else up every day.

## The Rearview Mirror

Don't look back! It's not the choices you've made or the tragedy you've endured. It's setting your eyes on the target ahead, living in acceptance and carving out a better life for yourself. The sky is the limit!

## Base

If you lined up every coach of every sport and asked them all what the most fundamental building block of a good athlete is, they would overwhelmingly agree, the athlete's "stance." I'll bet you're a bit surprised by this. It's not size, athletic ability, speed, or intelligence. Picture in your mind the following:

1. A shortstop's position on a ground ball.

2. A hockey goalie defending his goal.

3. A wrestler ready to strike a weak leg of an opponent.

4. A defender in basketball hawking the ball handler.

5. A linebacker anticipating the snap of the football.

6. A boxer, arm cocked, ready to deliver a final blow.

All of these athletes have a common trait: a fundamental, balanced stance. It provides for stability, strength, quickness, maneuverability, and consistency. Think of tennis, skiing, track, soccer, and volleyball. They all reflect the importance of proper stance, which I call a base. A base is necessary for sports but also plays a major part in a man's life, describing your balance, consistency, demeanor, as well as your physical, emotional, and mental equilibrium.

Having a base indicates a man of principle with beliefs that cannot be swayed or compromised. Just as an athlete who demonstrates a poor base will be unstable and off balance, a man's life will reflect the same. A popular slogan that holds true says, "If you don't stand for something, you'll fall for anything."

A man who's not afraid to disagree with another in principle or belief has a base. A man who will stand tall for what he believes, especially when unpopular, has a base. A man who is not swayed to casually change his mind has a base. Remembering who you are and where you come from is having a base.

# Conclusion

Everybody says they want to write a book but I'm sure very few ever do. There are so many facets to the art of constructing a book. By now there are a few things I've figured out but I still have a long way to go.

The process started in the most unlikely place; the daunting hallways of a Federal Medium Security Prison. I began by just pouring out emotions, anger, frustration, with a great deal of soul searching. My handwriting is horrible but I was able to decipher it well enough to get my diary typed. About 1,500 handwritten pages were needed to make up the final prison project of 305 typed pages. I would then journey to the library and make copies to send home, little by little. The chance of something happening to the original manuscript was high, so I took no chances. The book writing process is that - indeed; a process. Very little of those 305-pages actually made it into this book. The themes are present, but not the actual text.

There were struggles for sure during the writing and editing processes. As explained in an early chapter, my battle with FOMO (*FOMO* is defined as: "the uneasy and sometimes all-consuming feeling that you're missing out") extended into this project. Trying to write a perfect book should never be the goal, but many times I went back to change, delete, or add new content trying to put the perfect shine on it. It was very important to me that my life was used as the backdrop for the real intention of the book, and that is to examine and challenge others on their own adversity, decision-making, and healthy approach to moving through their storms of life. A book about only 'me' may have been boring, but written in the context of how my trials can challenge and help others is the primary goal. It's my hope that was accomplished here.

So many things were not included within these pages, notably, family relationships and memories. I'm hopeful there will be a time for a book filled with stories about my parents and siblings. So many friends and supporters are not included due to the topic and flow of the book, but as *they* say, *You know who you are.* I'm sure there will also be a place for the hundreds on my list who have been there to catch me through so many experiences, and continue to do so. The Lord blessed me with an incredible family and a slew of comrades in which to share life.

Most days are full of gratitude, hope, forward moving with a touch of remorse and sadness. Shedding the past has been hard for me but I allow it to last but a second. When I allow it to define me, then I've given anyone power to do the same. Knowing who we truly are and living in a way that exhibits our own true definition is a blessing.

One of the best questions I've ever heard goes like this, *Who are you and how would anyone know*? A person could spend an entire lifetime pondering and answering this question. Our essence is the *who* of our existence. It's not the job, the awards, the bank account, or our status. Realizing who we are takes us down to the deepest darkest place because that's where the truth really lives. I'm challenged every day to answer that question and move forward.

Addictions are a tricky reminder of how my decisions can alter everything. There is always some reminder that I'm one drink or one click away from ruin. It's daunting but realistic. To a degree, we all can say that. With time-tested strategies in place, I've been able to handle the ghosts of the past over the last 14 years. But I also know that the moment you begin to feel cured or over the hump, it's your addict that is doing pushups in the corner. Satan strikes where we feel we are invincible and have the world by the tail. Putting strategies in place and realizing there is an addiction under the surface is a balancing act but due to the professionals who have helped me, guided me, and challenged me, my armor is in place.

The fourth quarter of life will be full of surprises, no doubt. I could never say, *I've seen it all*, though surely, my experiences are many. I look forward to warm relationships with my family, especially with my mom, Nan. Friends are always there in need but a phone call can spark new hopes and dreams for the future. Todd calls on the 18th, Burk frets over the name of our band, Bear reminds me of that Bigfoot is still out there, Andy leaves a "HAP" voicemail, Jay adds a new guitar phenom to All Dixie Rock, Hone threw another Red Grange at the boys, Orv needs coffee, and my coaching buddies share one of thousands of memories from our days on the hardwood and highway. Never will I allow my friendships to fade into the busyness of life. "Friends forever", that's what my mom told me.

Professionally, I have goals that I'm committed to reaching. To the best of my ability the theme will be centered around others; a sense of this world needing a hug, a handwritten note, or compassion. What a shame to have lived through life and its hurdles to this point and not share it with others. In basketball, not sharing the ball is selfishness. The same is true for life. Life is about our relationships and how our experiences can continue to be a gift to our fellow humanity.

This book has been a gift and has helped me in so many ways. These words serve as an accomplishment to me, but more importantly, they reaffirm that no matter where we find ourselves – there is always a way out. Even in a prison cell we can be free, hopeful, pouring out encouragement and compassion for others.

Thus far, my life has taught me that there is no situation too drastic to keep us from reaching out for help. What we don't want to do many times is exactly the thing we must do. Life is meant to be shared and I'm blessed beyond belief to have known so many wonderful people. I thank God for providing me all I have needed and also for the daily reminders that I am weak and unable to do life alone. I am blessed!

# About the Author, Randy Brown

**Randy Brown, 2017**

For nearly 20 years Randy Brown worked with the country's finest coaches, including Basketball Hall of Famer, Lute Olson. Randy reached the highest level in men's college basketball and his NCAA Division I experience includes five regular season championships, two post-season tournament championships, five NCAA Tournaments, back-to-back Big 12 titles, and the 2000 Elite Eight. Four of his Arizona players have captured a total of 13 NBA Championships as players and coaches. His stops include the University of Arizona, Marquette University, Iowa State University, Miami of Ohio, University of North Dakota, Drake University and Stetson. Ten NBA players have benefitted from his coaching expertise, including Steve Kerr, current Golden State Warriors head coach, and Sean Elliott, National Player of the Year, 1988.

Randy's rise in the coaching world was matched by his dramatic plunge into the depths of depression after two of his children's deaths, prison, and a career lost forever. But Randy is not one to stay down when life's adversities push him against the ropes. He has since created an extensive world-wide coach mentoring program, Elite Coach Mentoring. Over 100 coaches have reached their coaching goals working with Randy. The Iowa Player Development Academy, located in Central Iowa, focuses on teaching players to play the right way.

His networking tree extends deep into the basketball world; within two degrees he can connect to virtually every college and NBA coach. Randy is an author, speaker, mentor, consultant, and networking expert as well as a certified Life Coach through CoachU. He also holds a position as an Emeritus Coach with the National Association of Basketball Coaches.

Randy's expertise in dealing with life's adversities provides a powerful platform for his presentation, "Rebound Forward." He delivers a one-two punch to audiences around the country through his keynote presentation in concert with his book of the same title, *Rebound Forward—How to Rebound from Life's Most Devastating Losses and Stay in the Game.*

Randy Brown has two daughters, Claire, 26 and Jane, 21, and resides in Ames, Iowa.

# How to Order

*Rebound Forward* can be purchased through Randy's online Store at http://randybrown.coach or through Amazon.com.

Really want to help me? Leave a review on Amazon.

Interested in bulk or corporate orders?
Contact Randy Brown directly.
Contact information:
Phone: 515-450-1966
Email: reboundforwardbook@gmail.com
Website: http://randybrown.coach

## Speaking

Please contact me regarding speaking engagements, interviews, or radio appearances.

Pass It On
If you were impacted by reading *Rebound Forward*, please share the word with friends, family, neighbors, and graduates.
Not a big reader? Buy a copy and gift it to a friend who may benefit from *Rebound Forward*.

CPSIA information can be obtained
at www.ICGtesting.com
Printed in the USA
LVHW020939191020
669133LV00012B/587